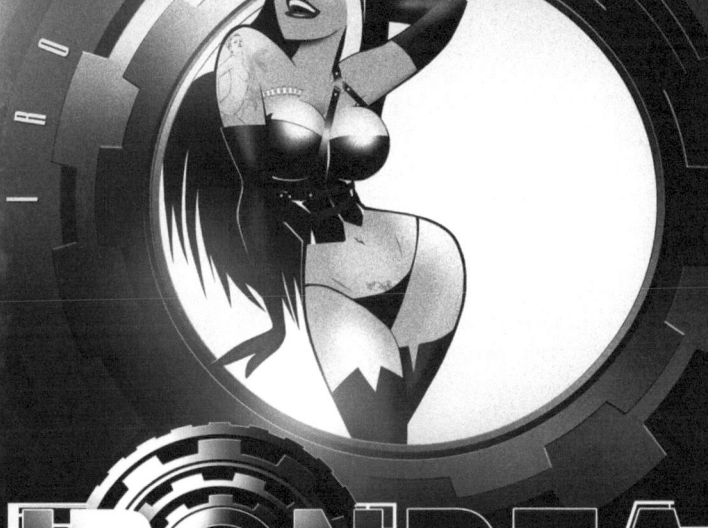

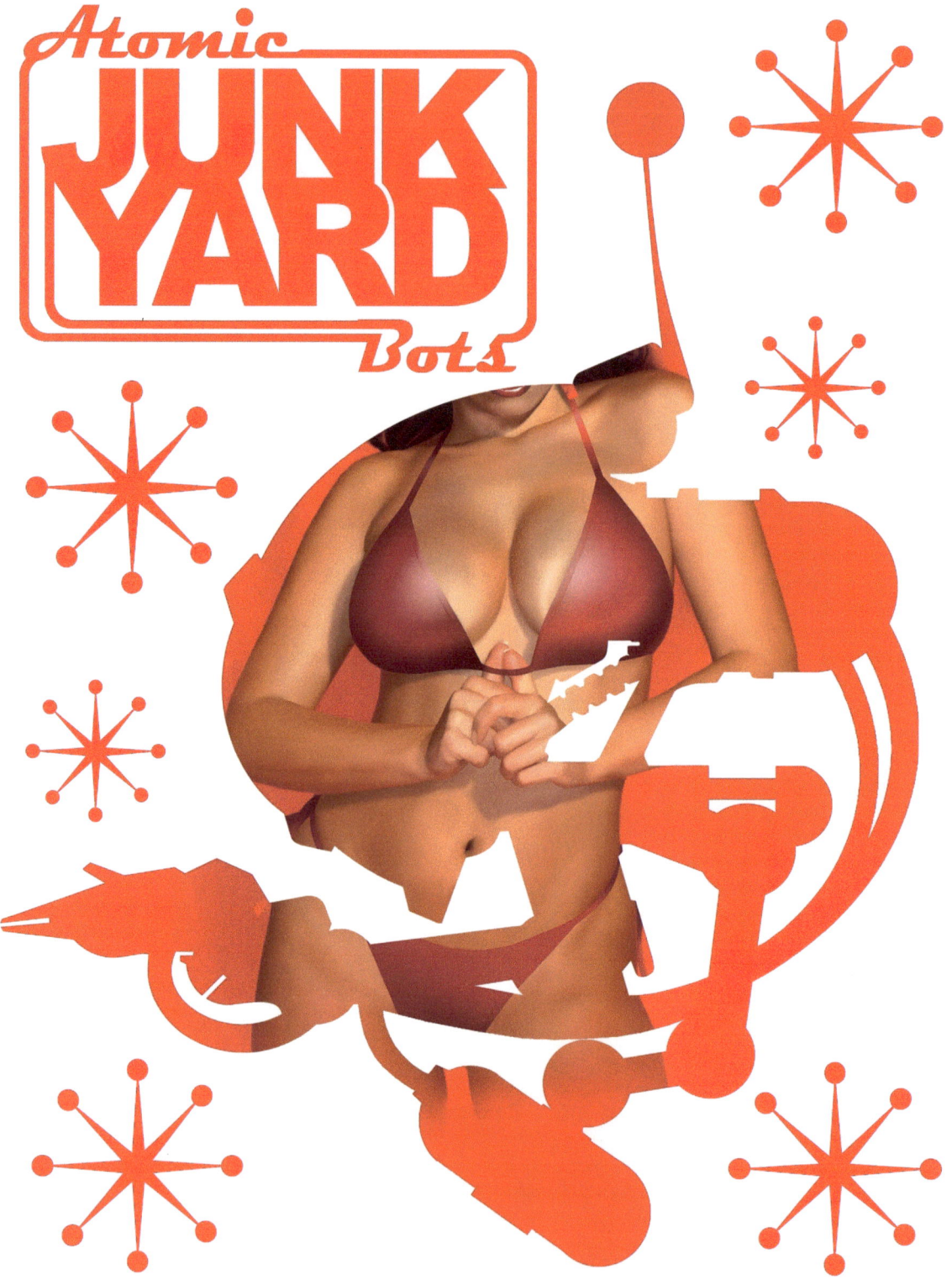

PARODY PIN-UP PORTFOLIO

ATOMIC JUNKYARD YARD BOTS is a trademark and copyright of IRON DEAD STUDIOS 2017. All rights reserved. Subject matters parodied are the sole property of their respective rights holders and are lampooned here under the guidelines of legal parody. This publication is for parody / humorous / lampoon purposes only. Art reference models Monique Dupree and Carmella Bing appear by permission. Any other resemblence to any other life form is purely coincidental. Please do not contact Iron Dead Studios is an attempt to get personal information of featured reference models. Do not contact Iron Dead Studios with requests to kidnap the aforementioned featured reference models for the sole purpose of cloning them in a trailer park. No joke. That actually happened. Some asshole actually proposed kidnapping Carmella Bing and cloning her with home-made equipment kept in a trailer park. I thought the guy was joking. He wasn't. If you happen to know someone who thinks like this, run. Run as far and as fast as you can. If you yourself think like that, please seek help and may God have mercy on your soul. Maintain grooviness at all times.

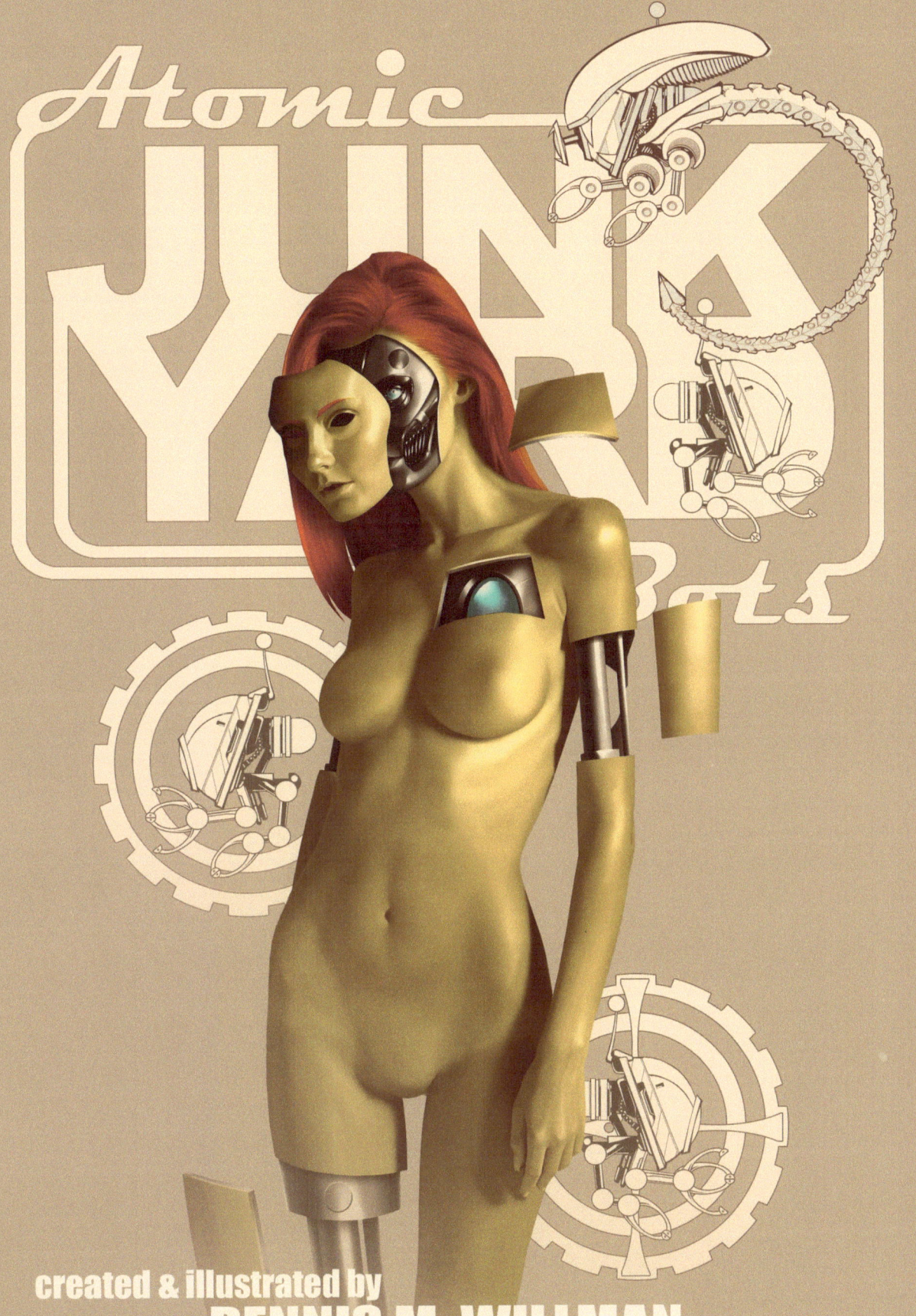

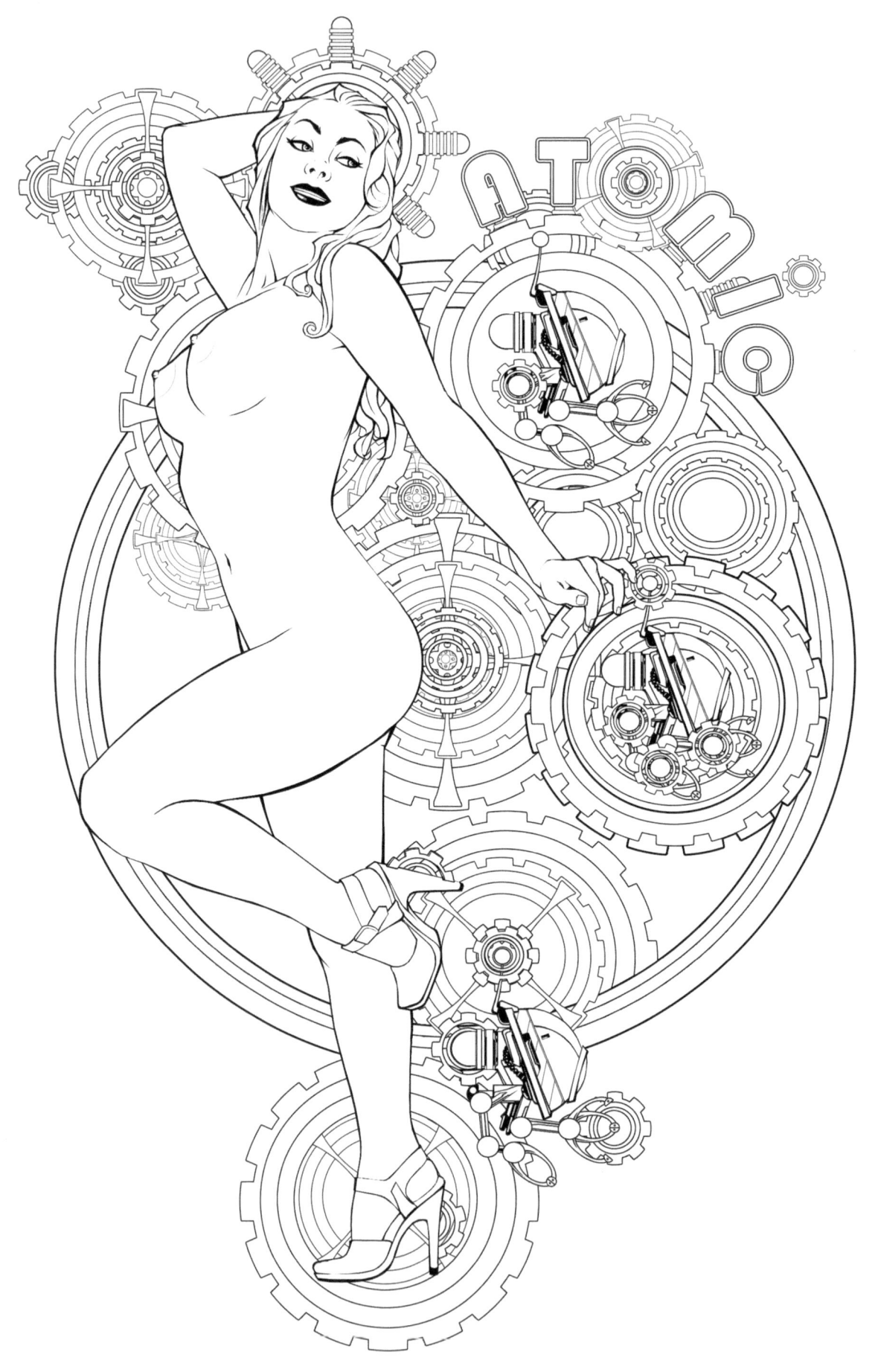

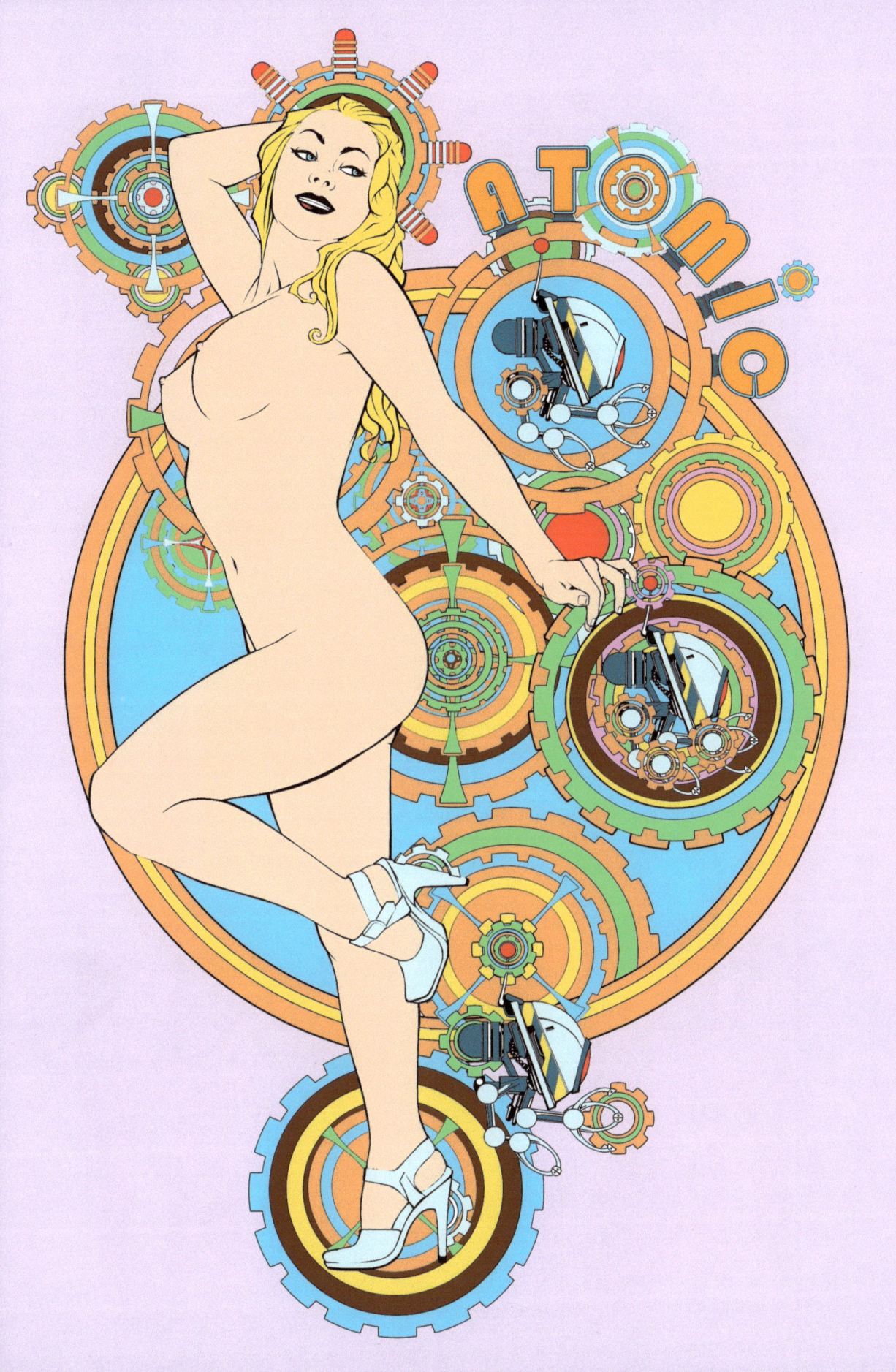

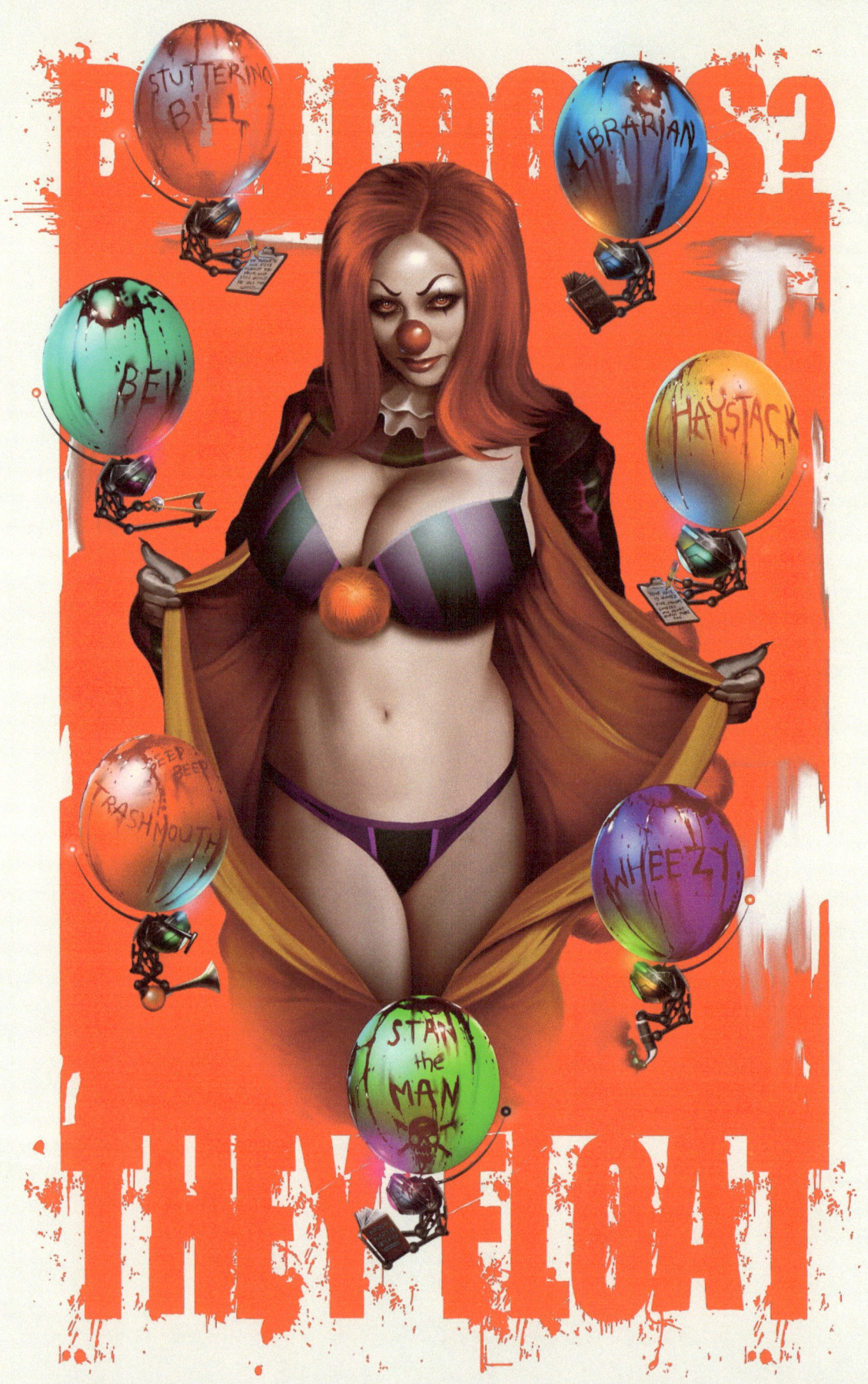

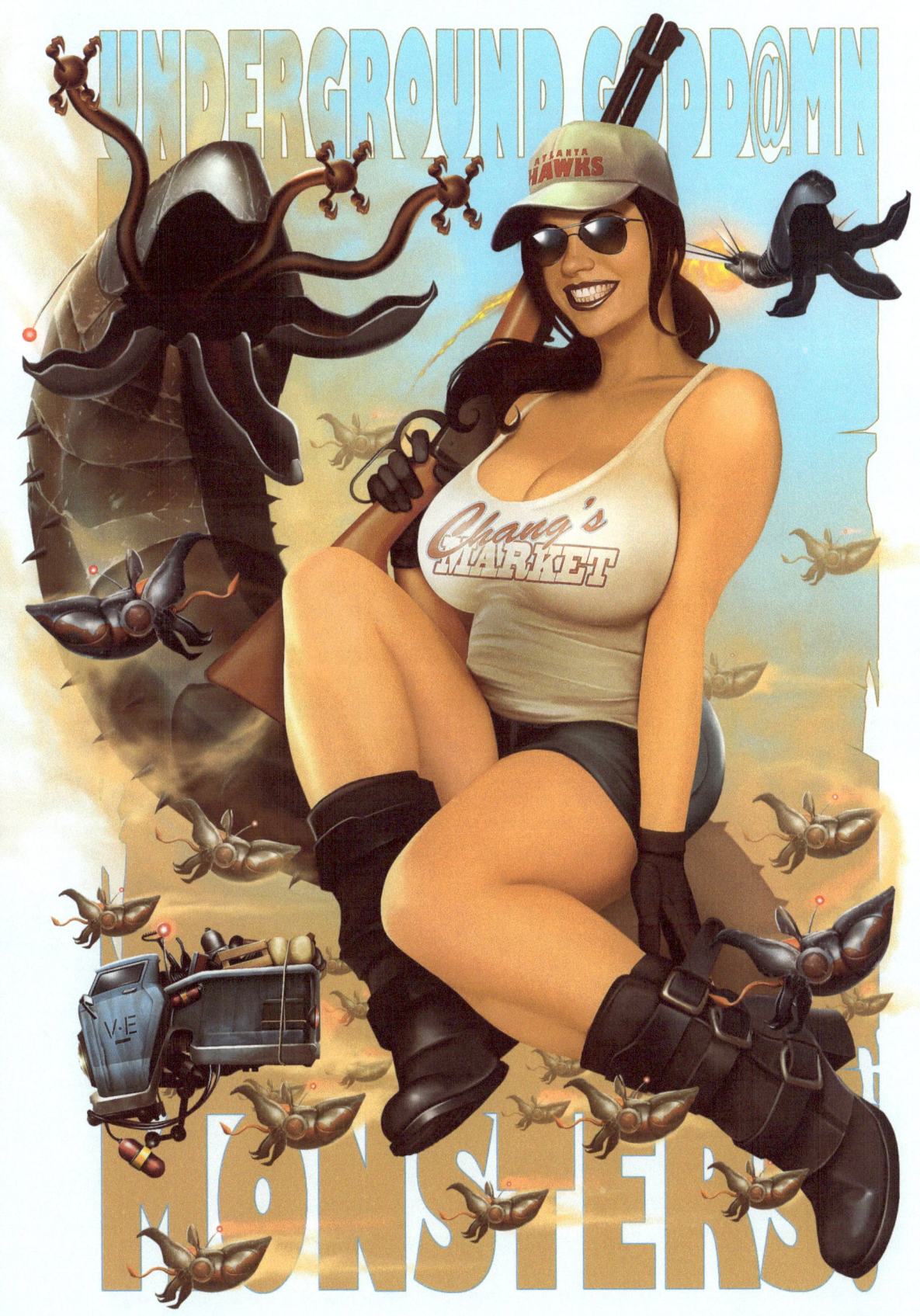

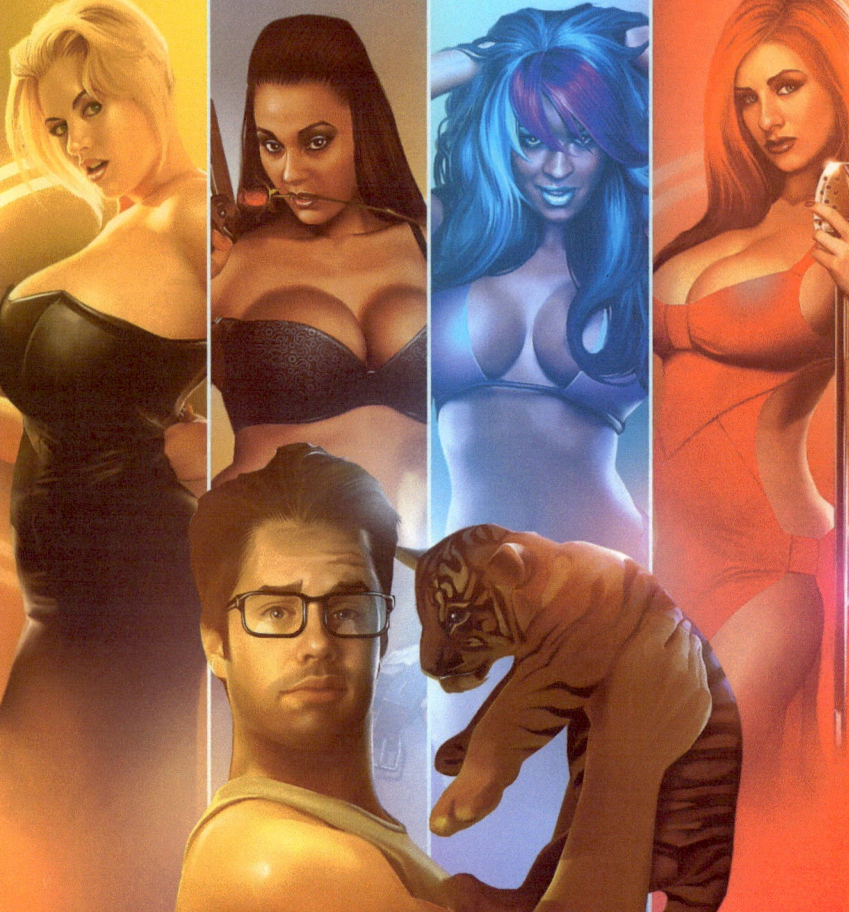

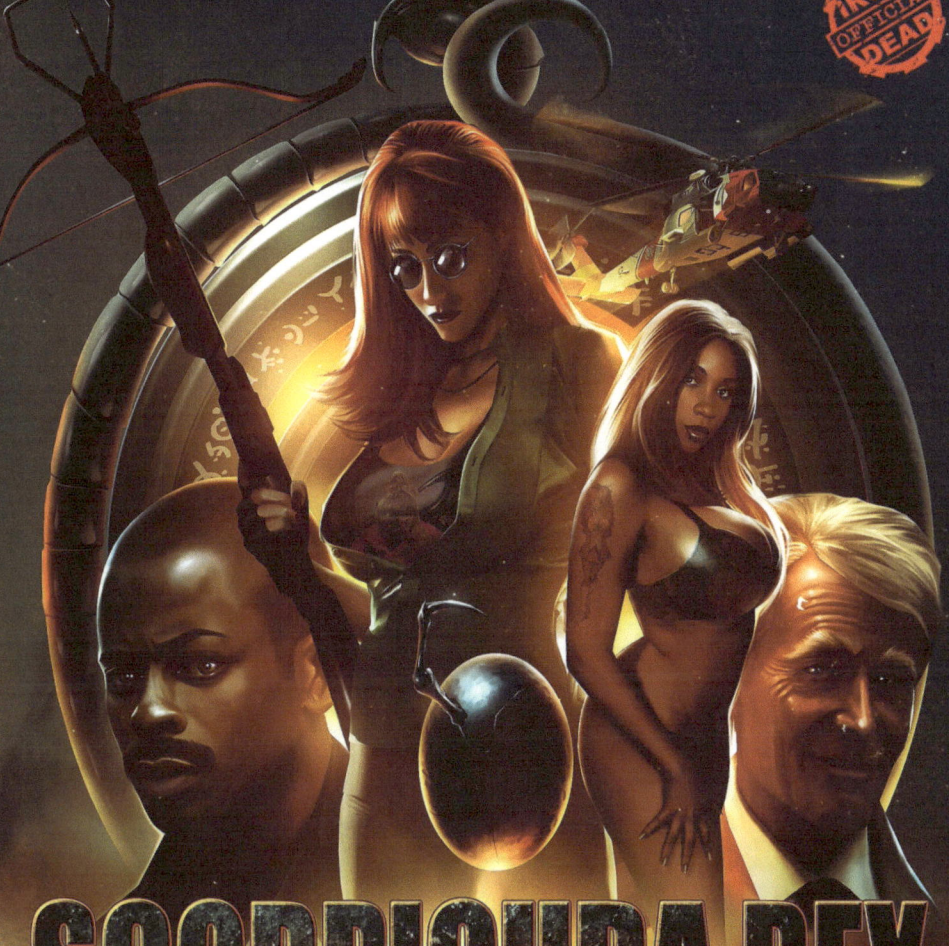

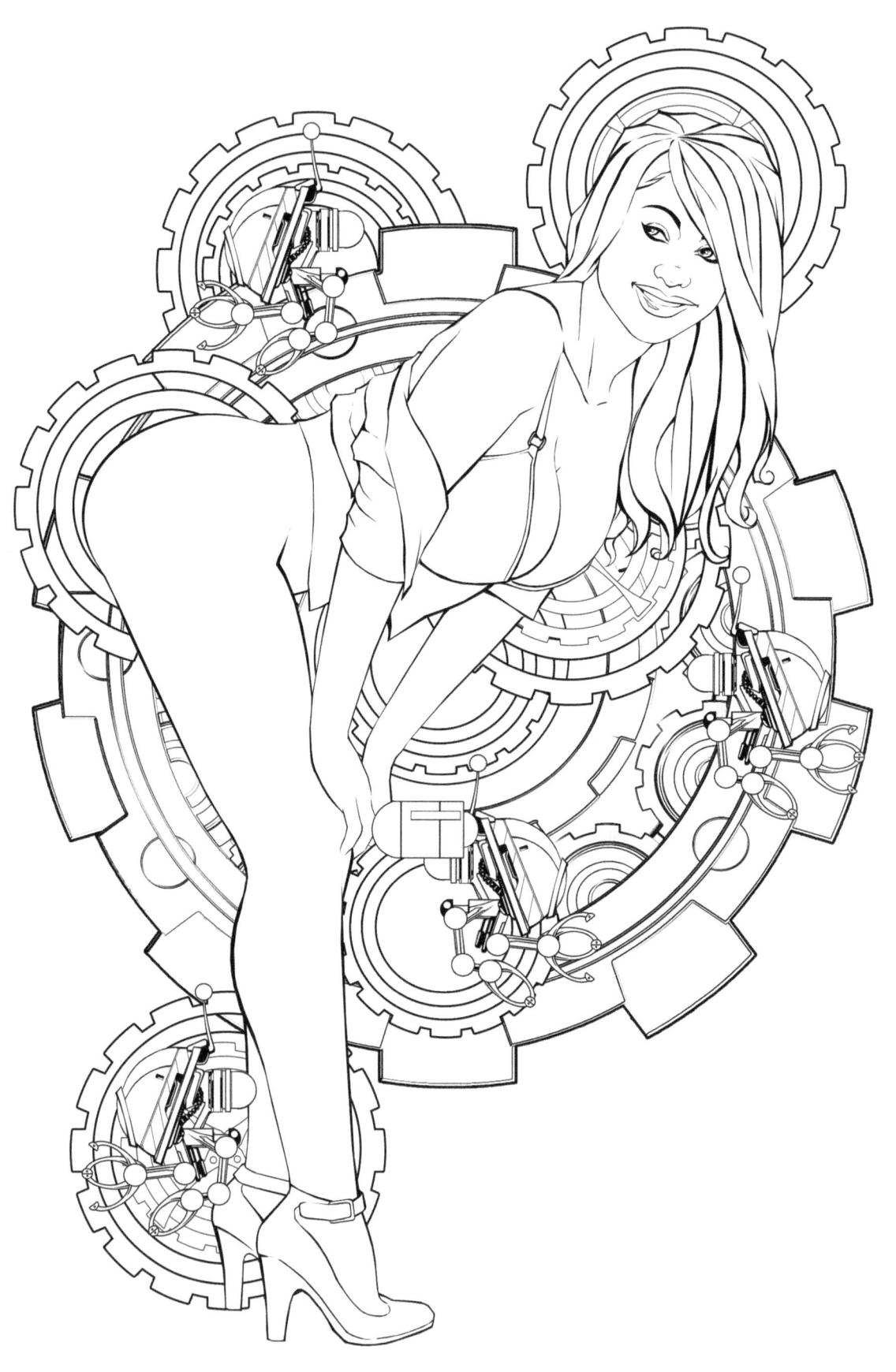

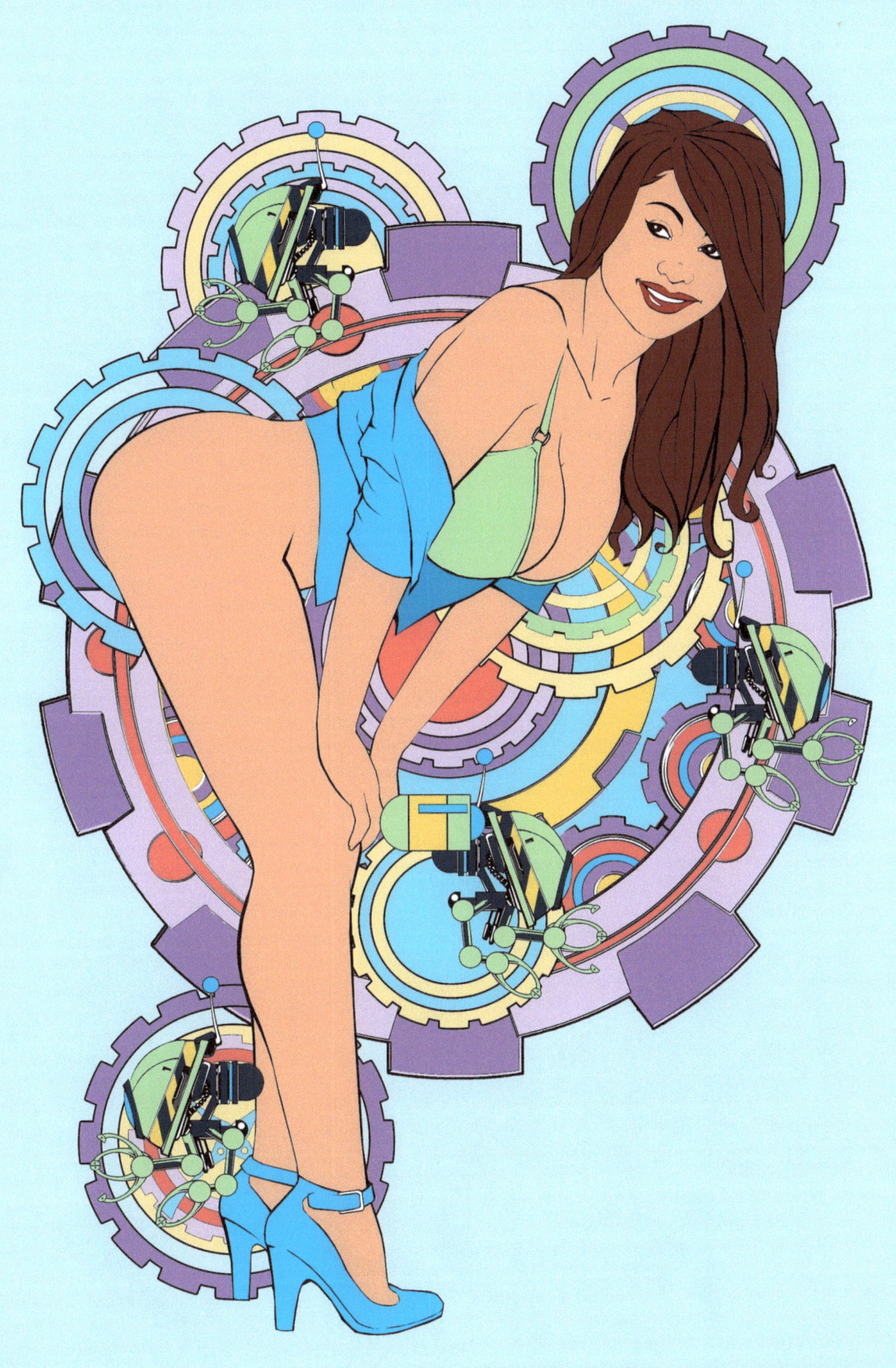

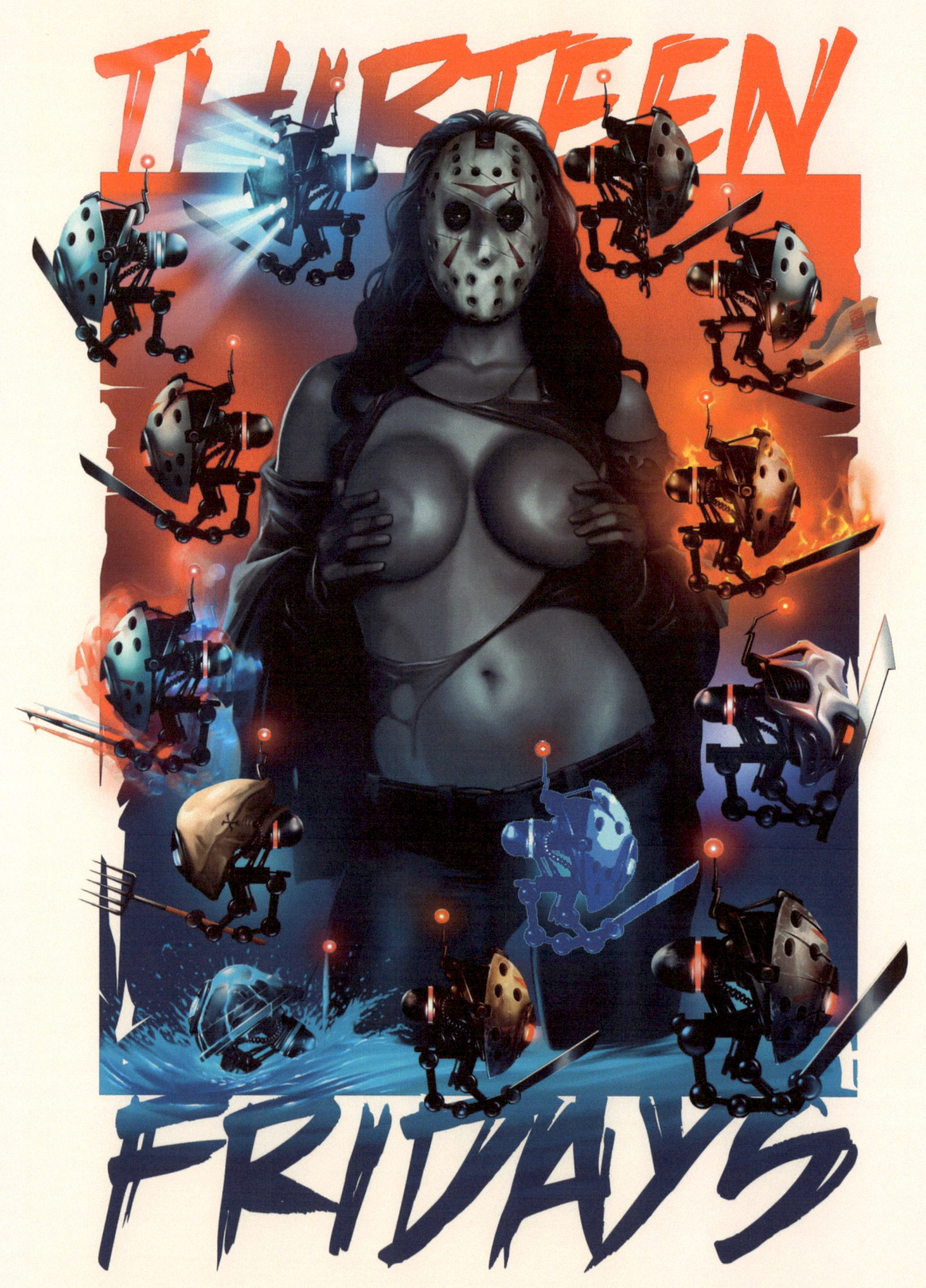

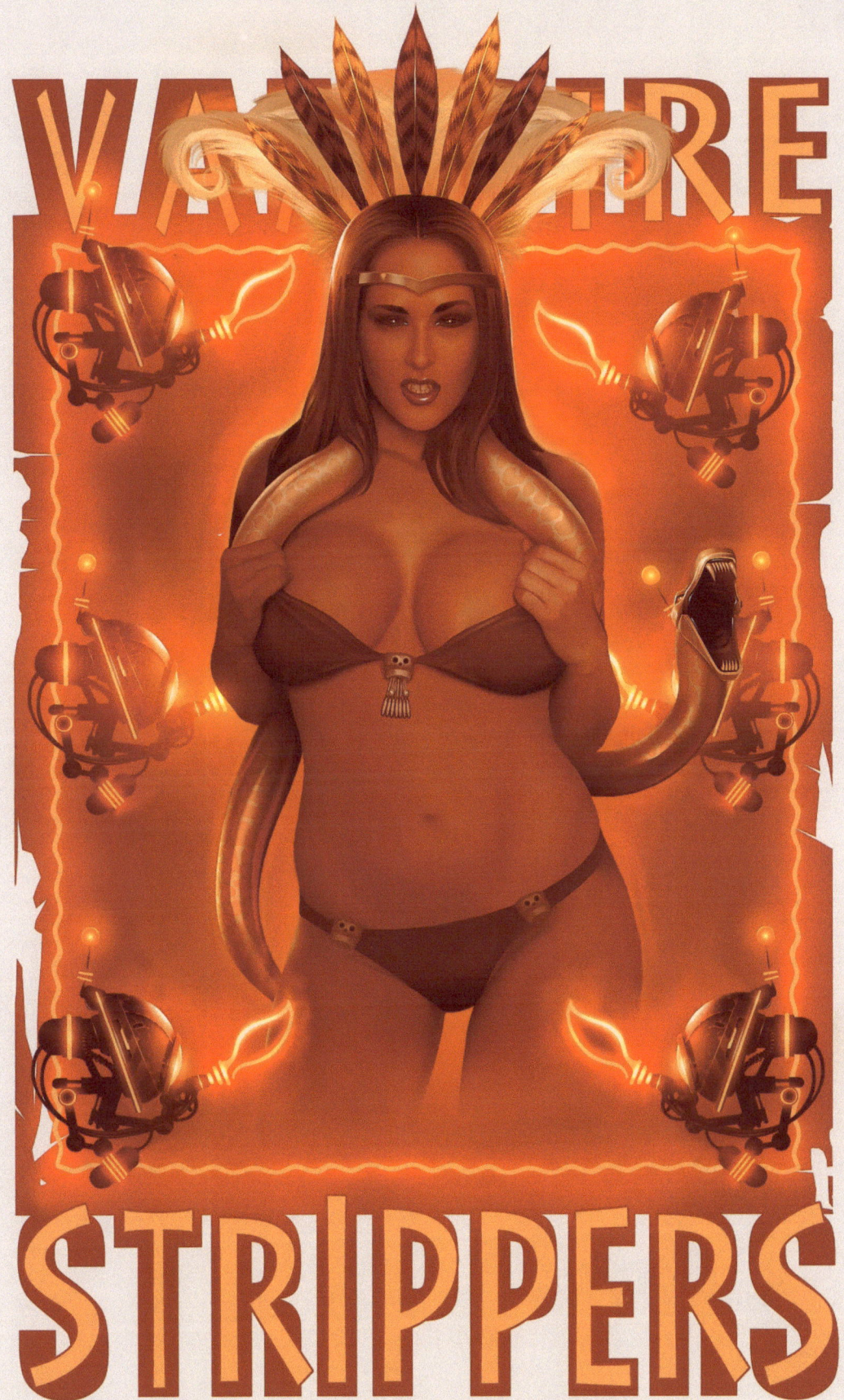

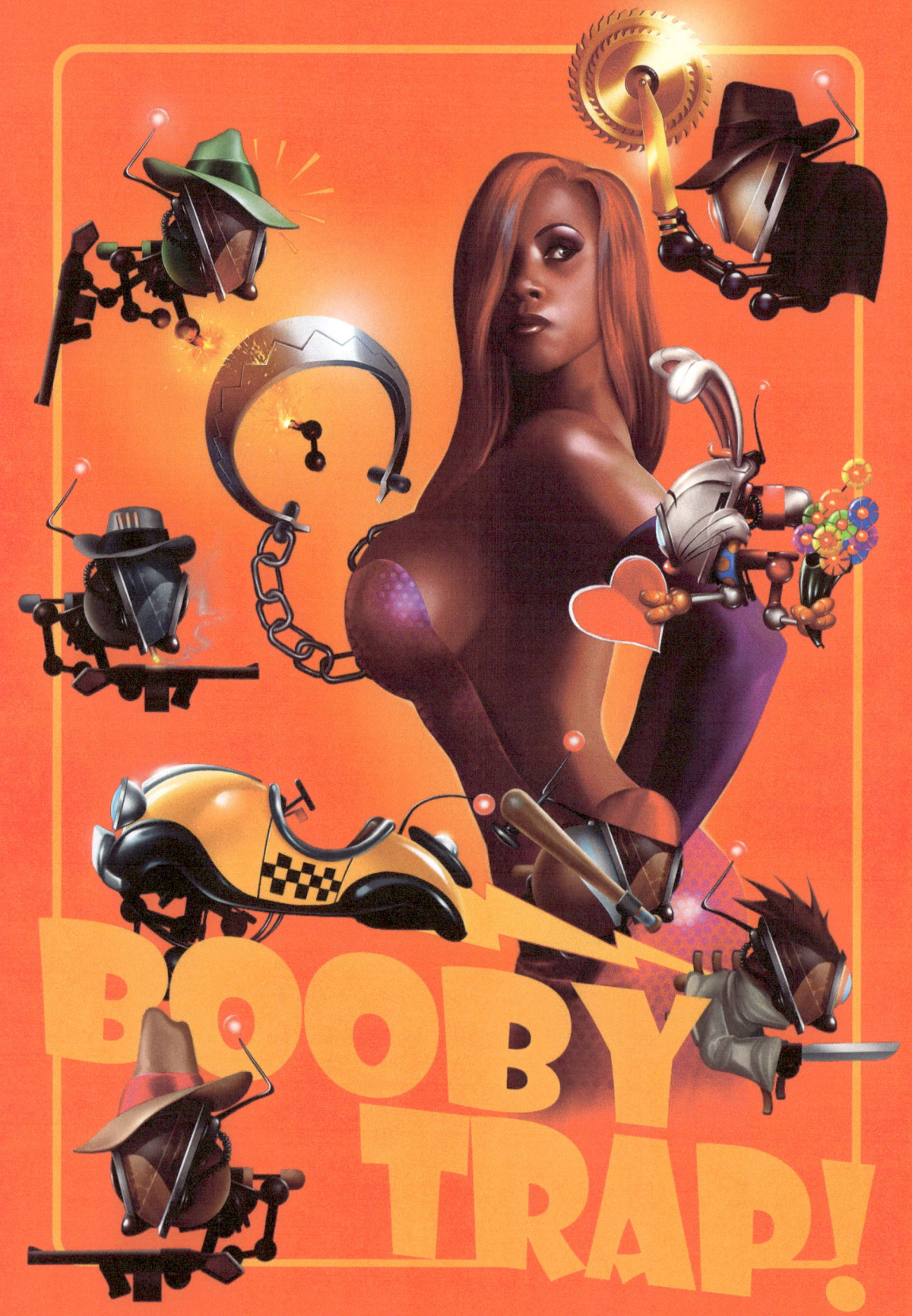

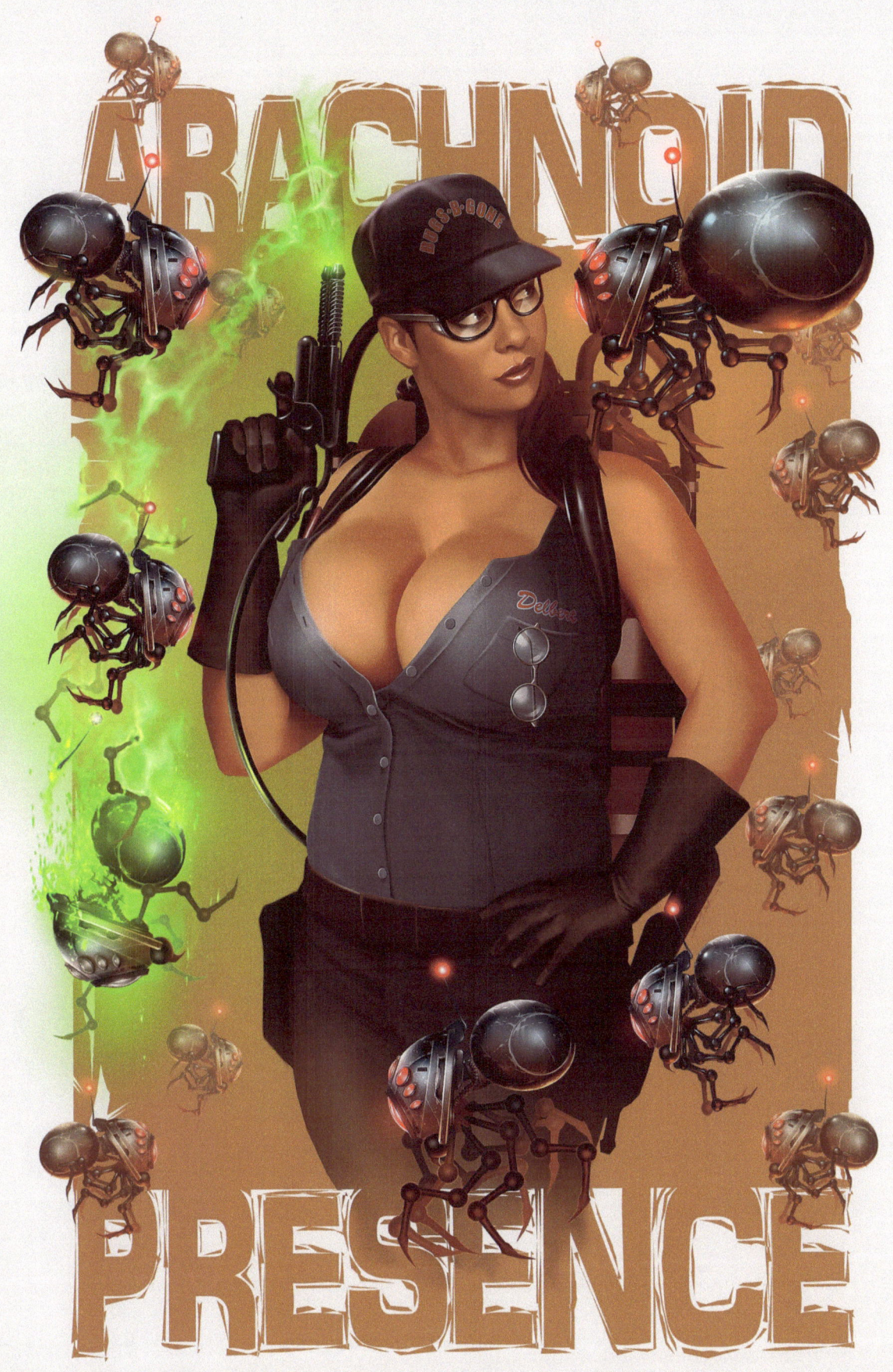

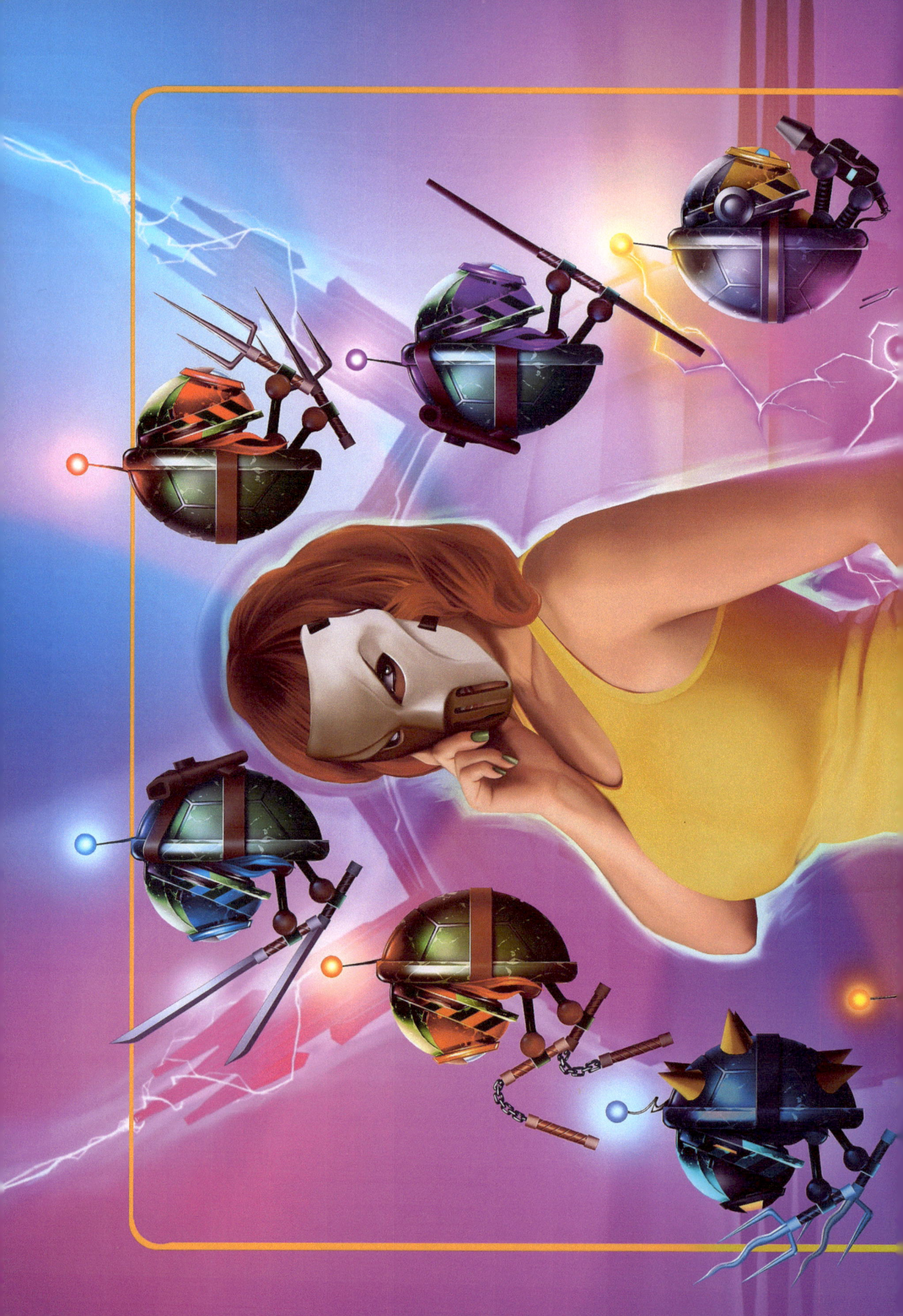

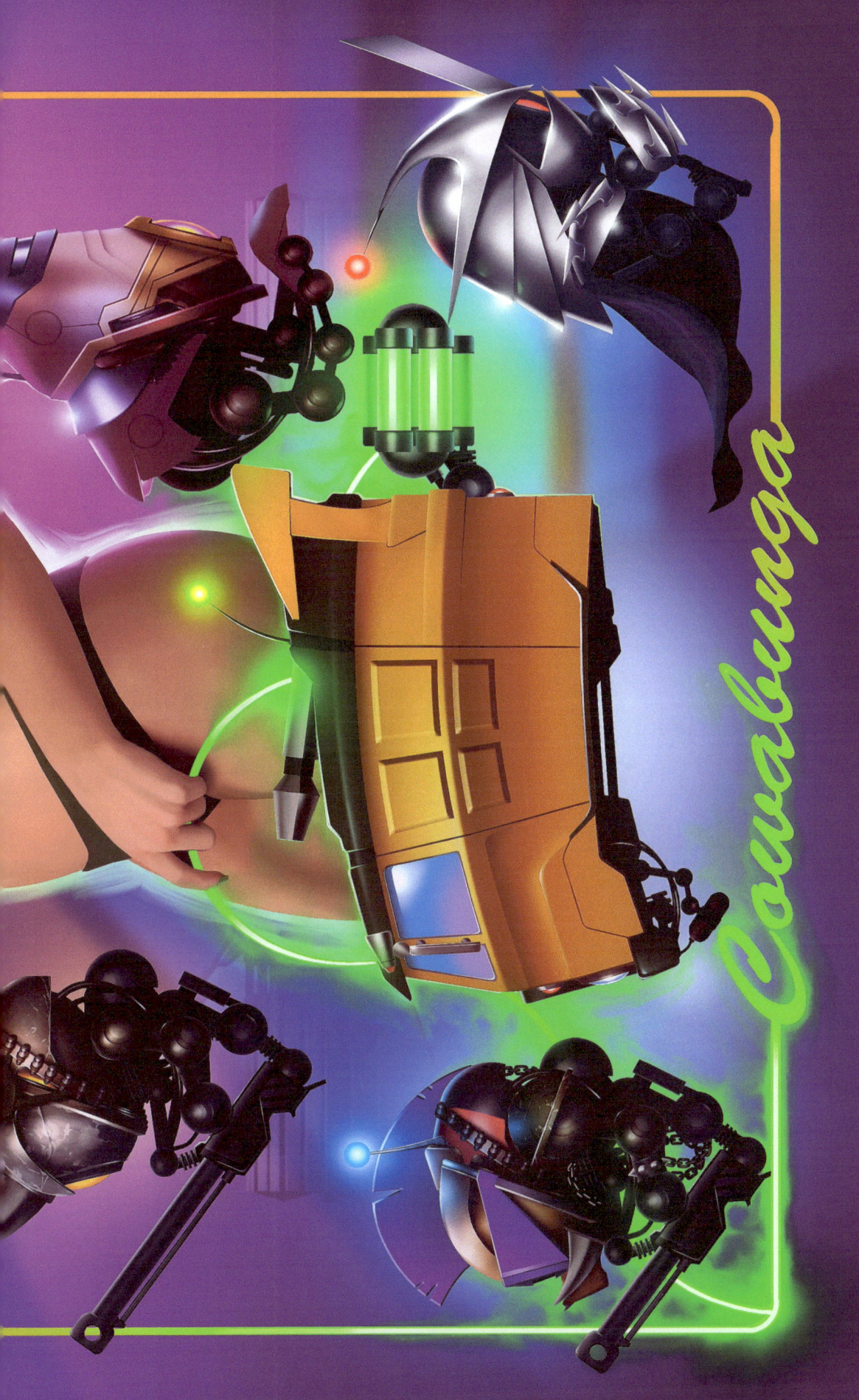

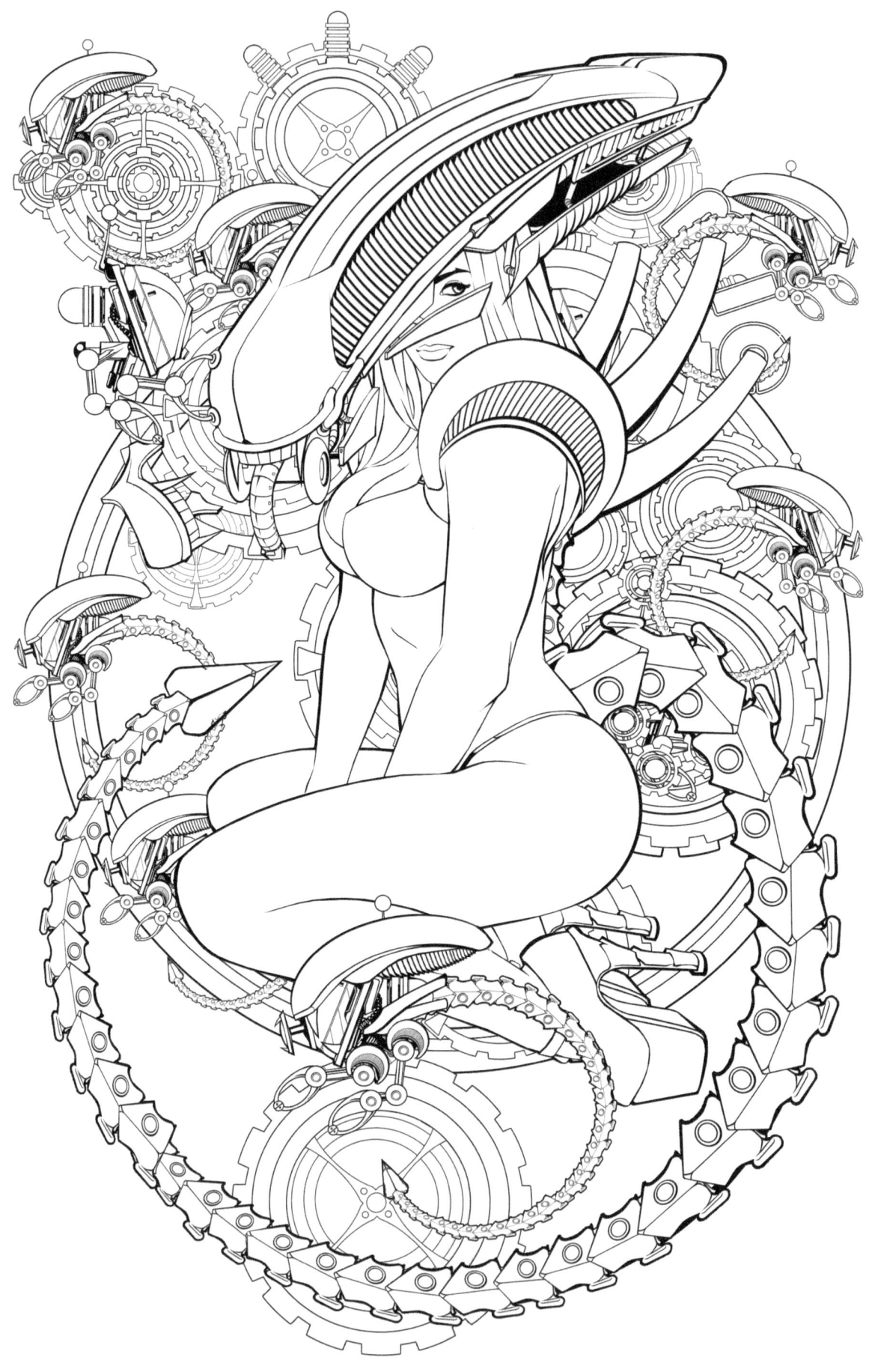

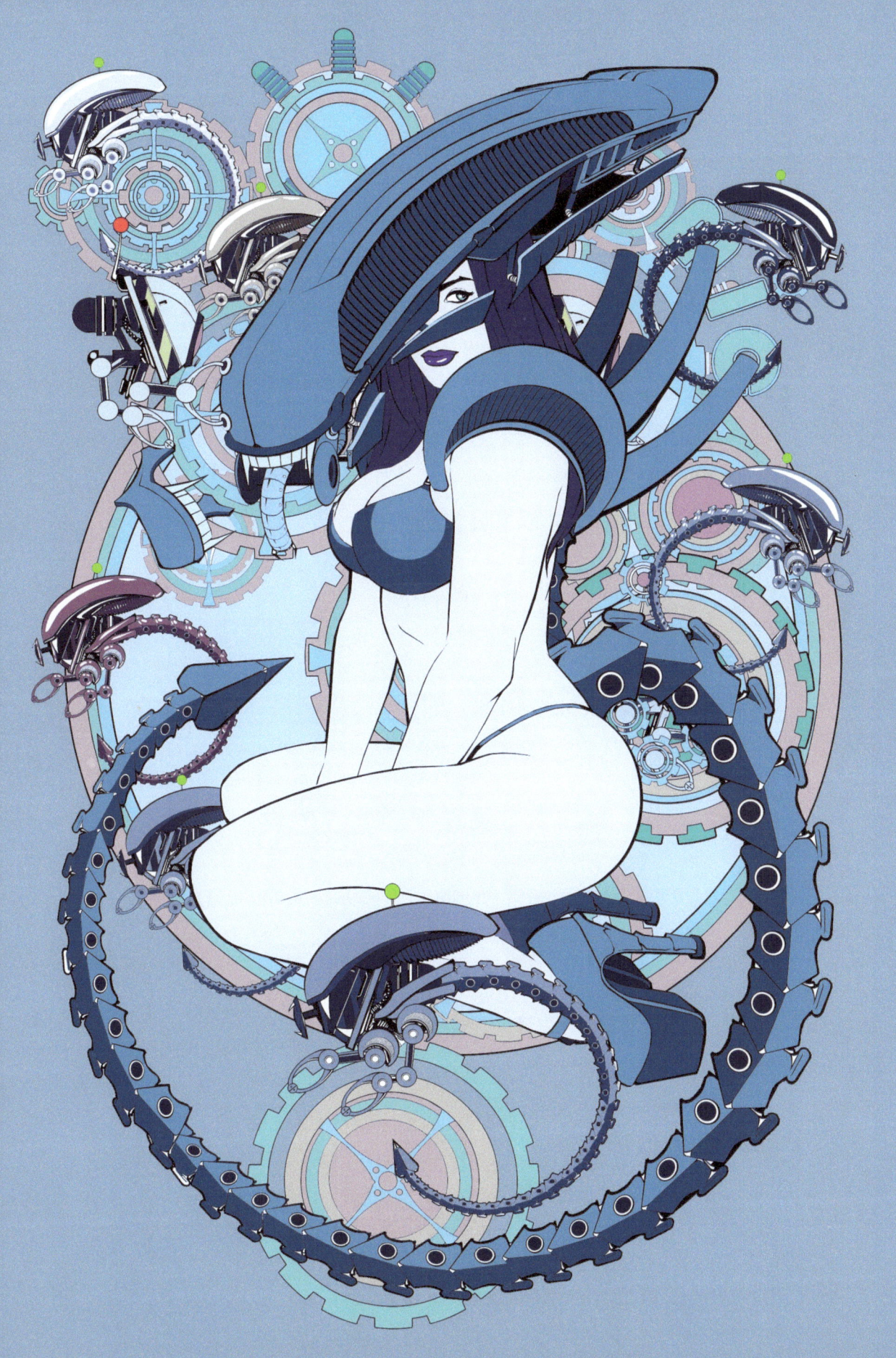

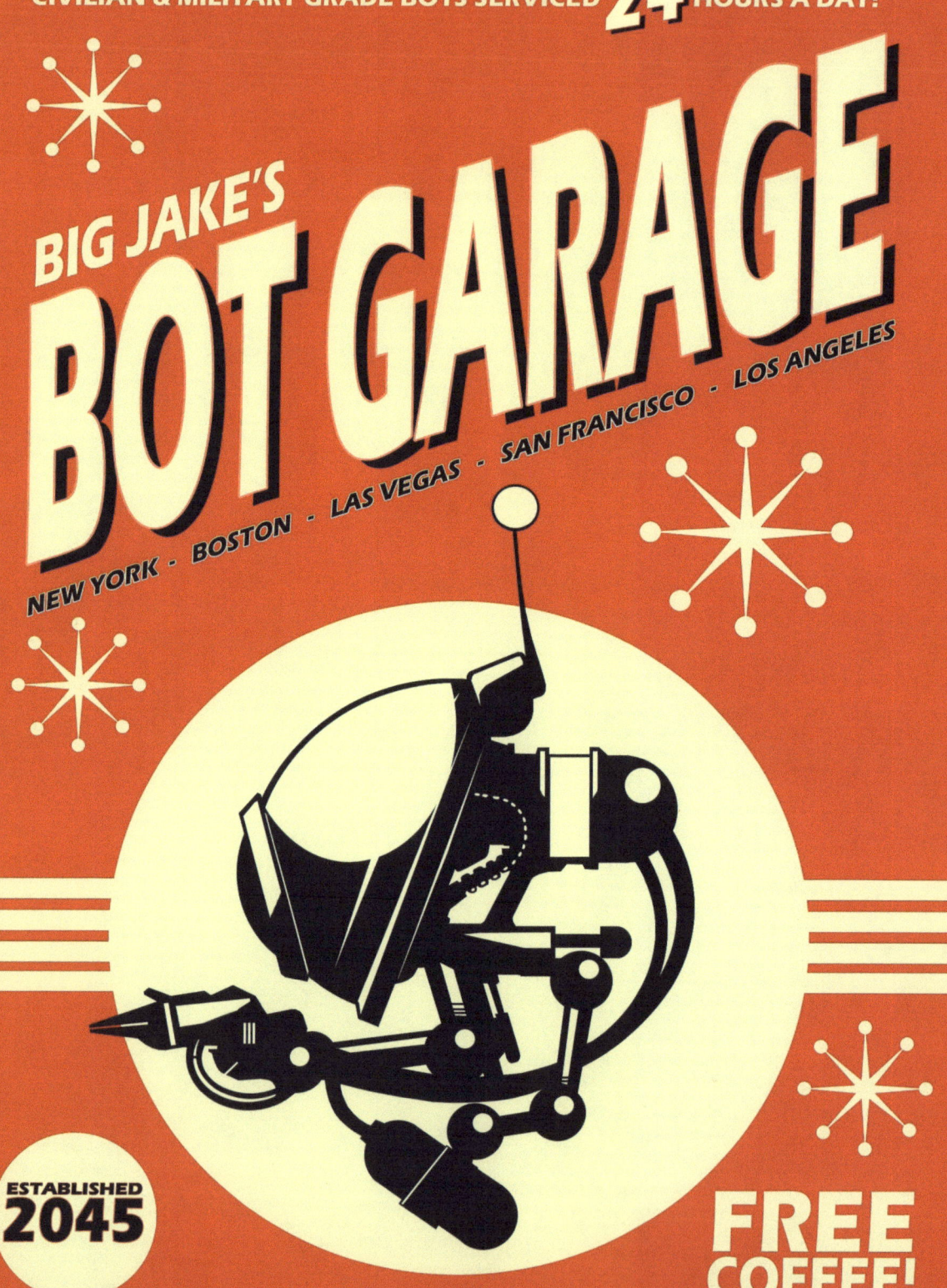

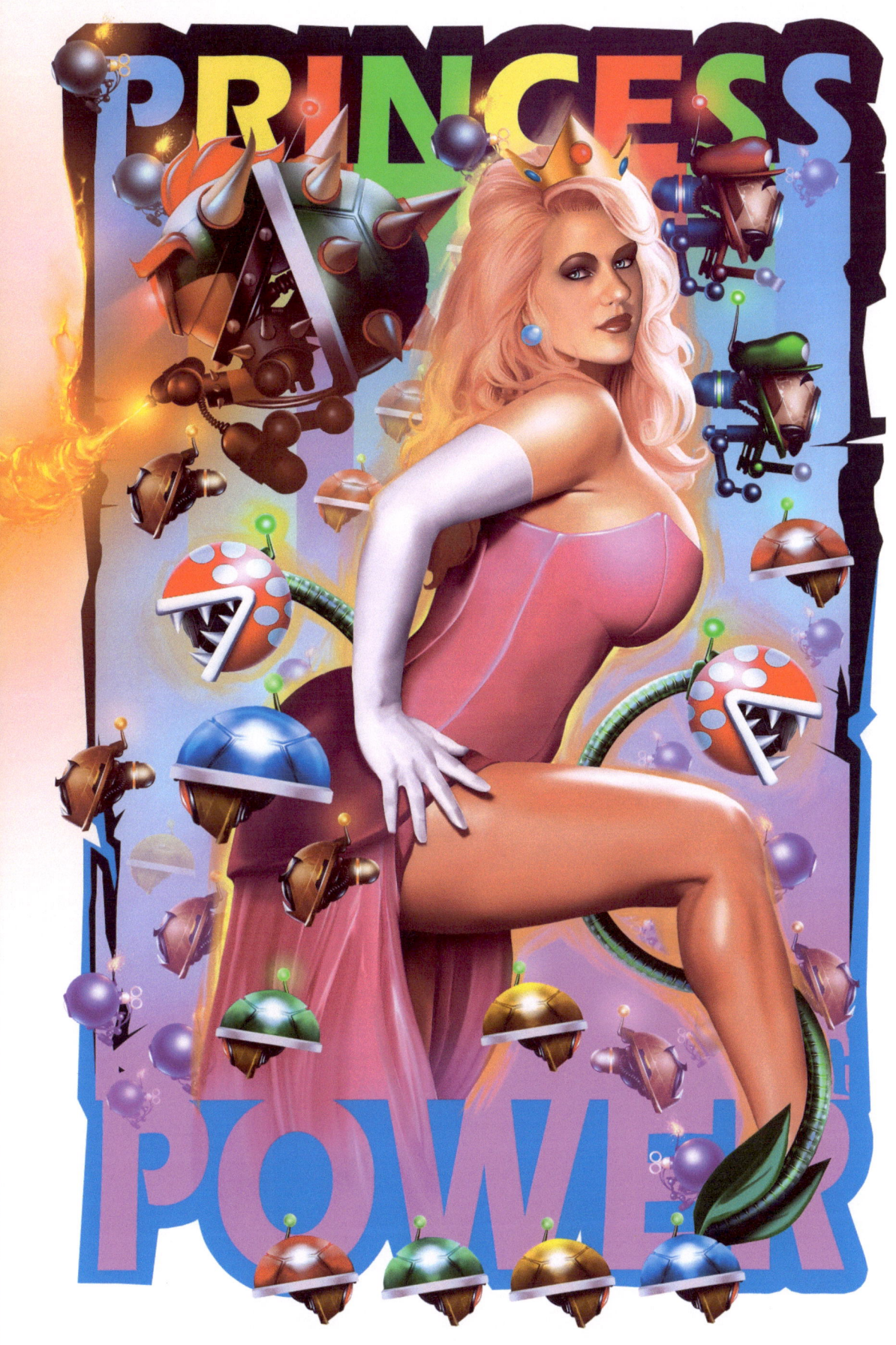

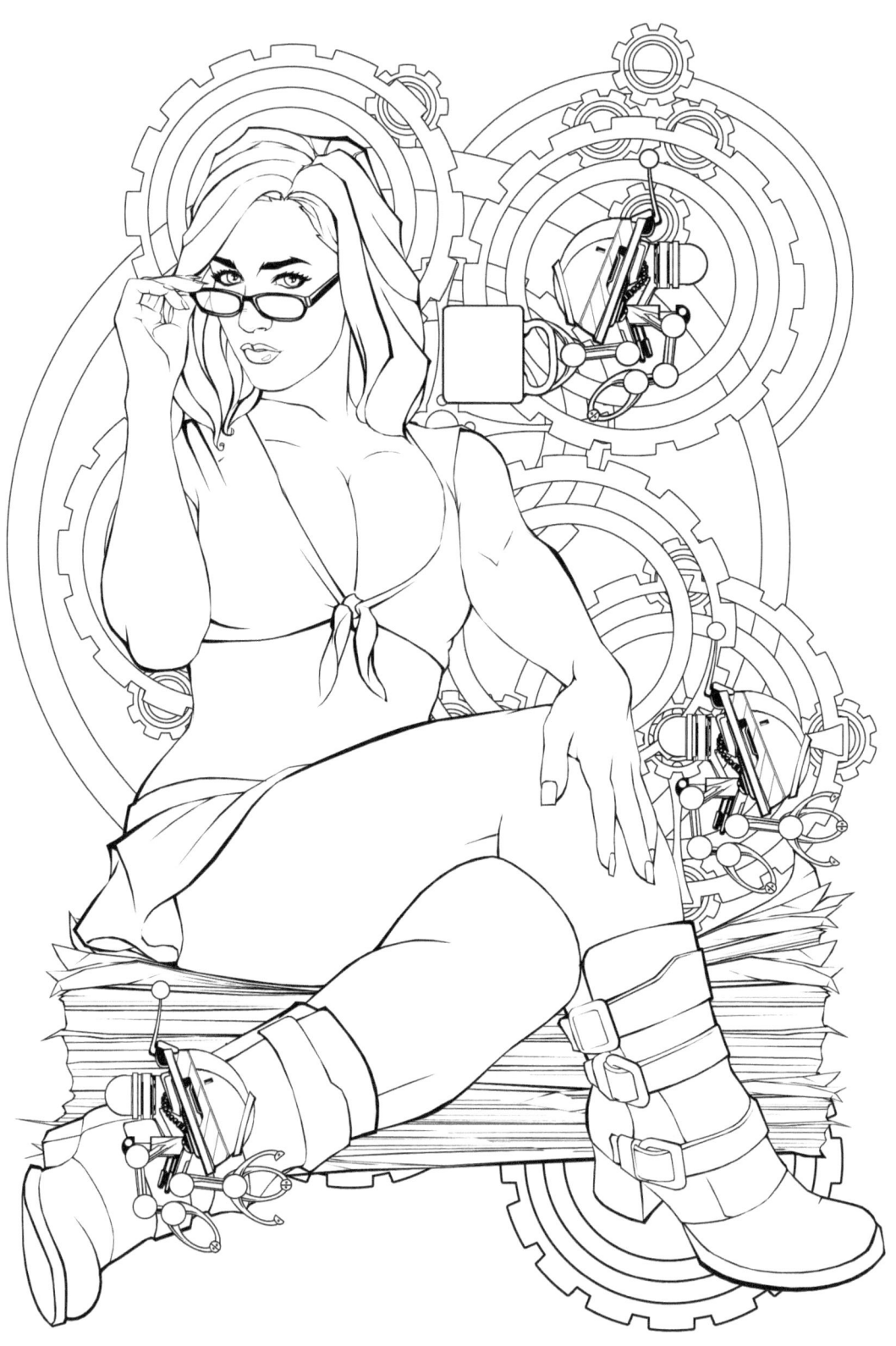

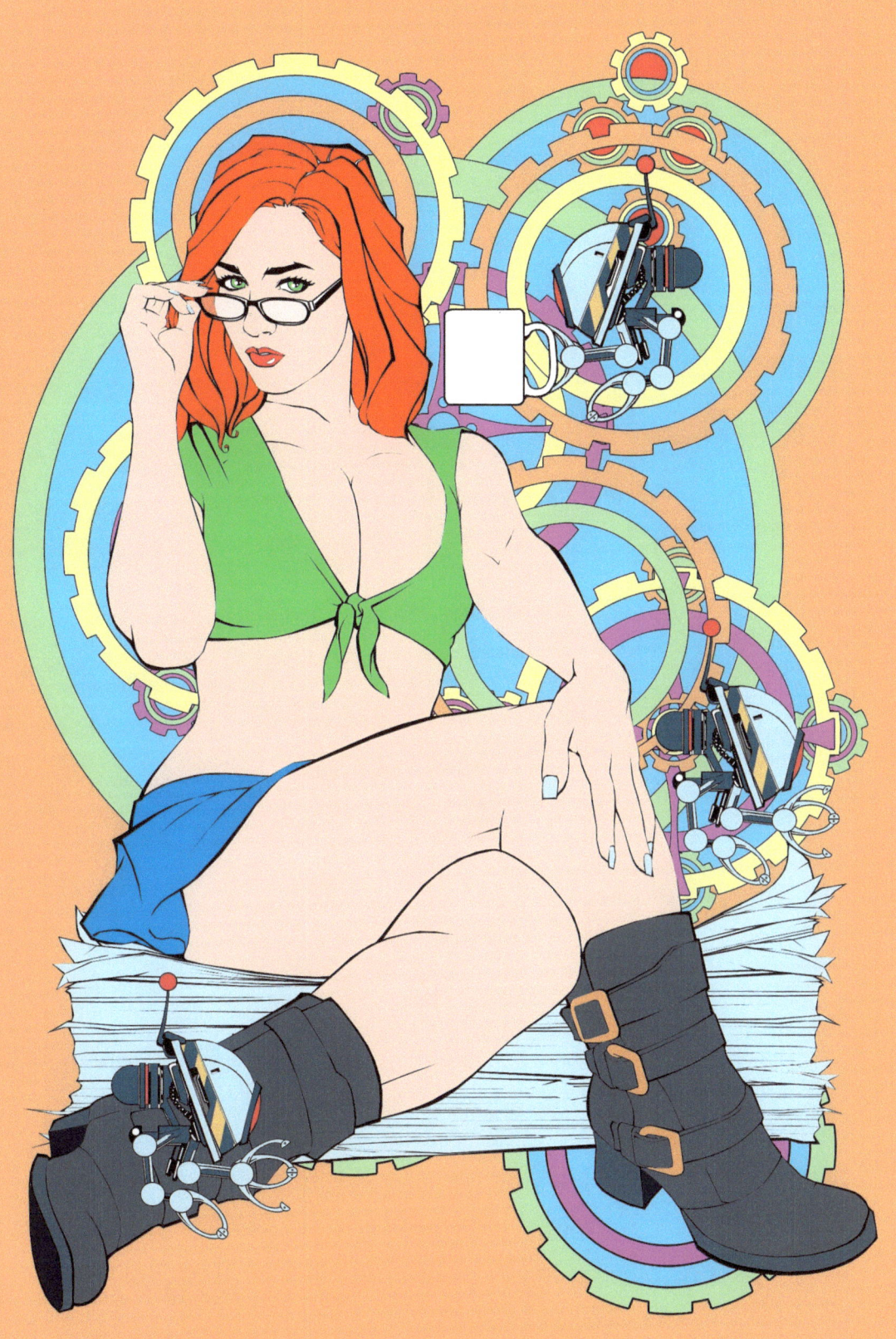

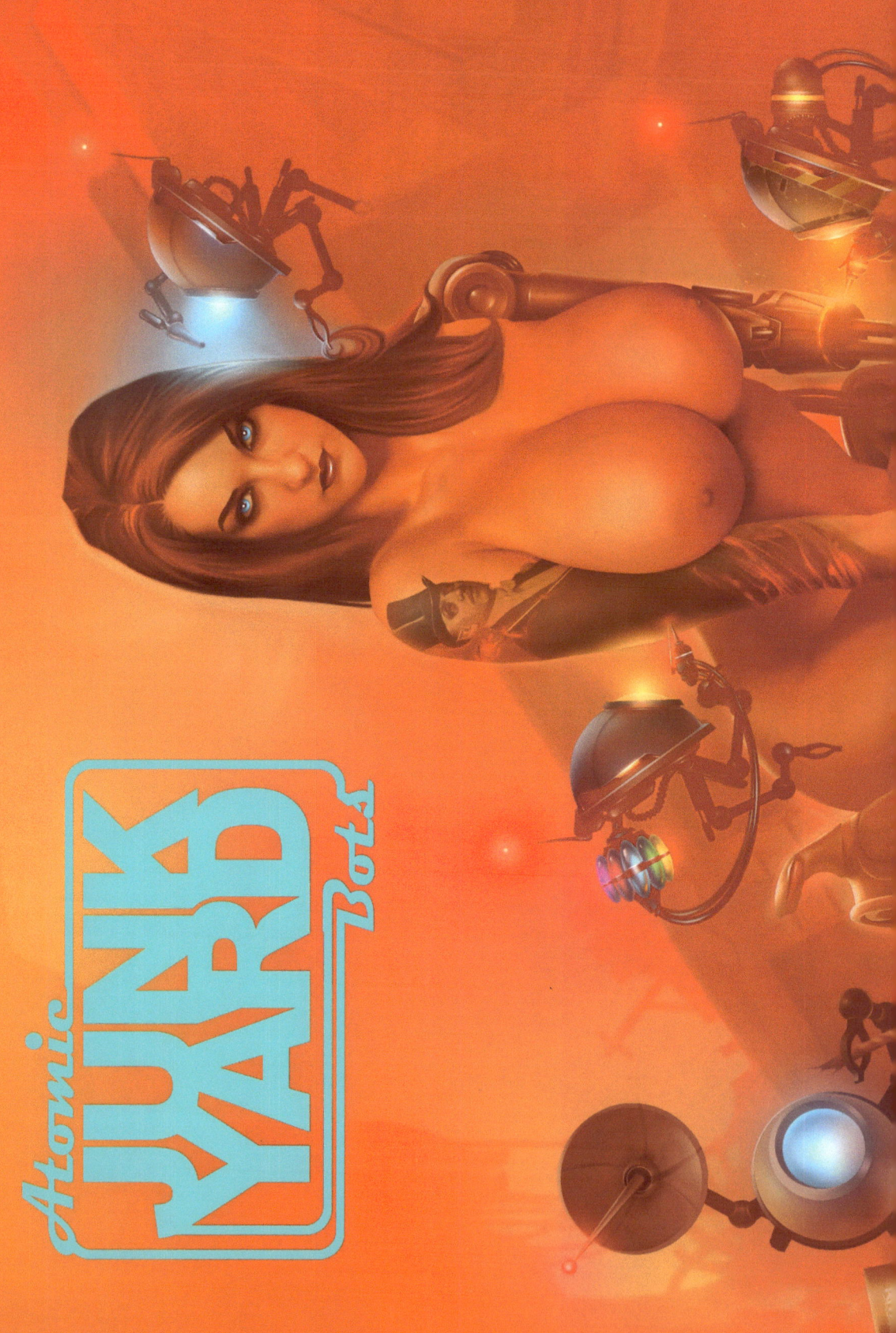

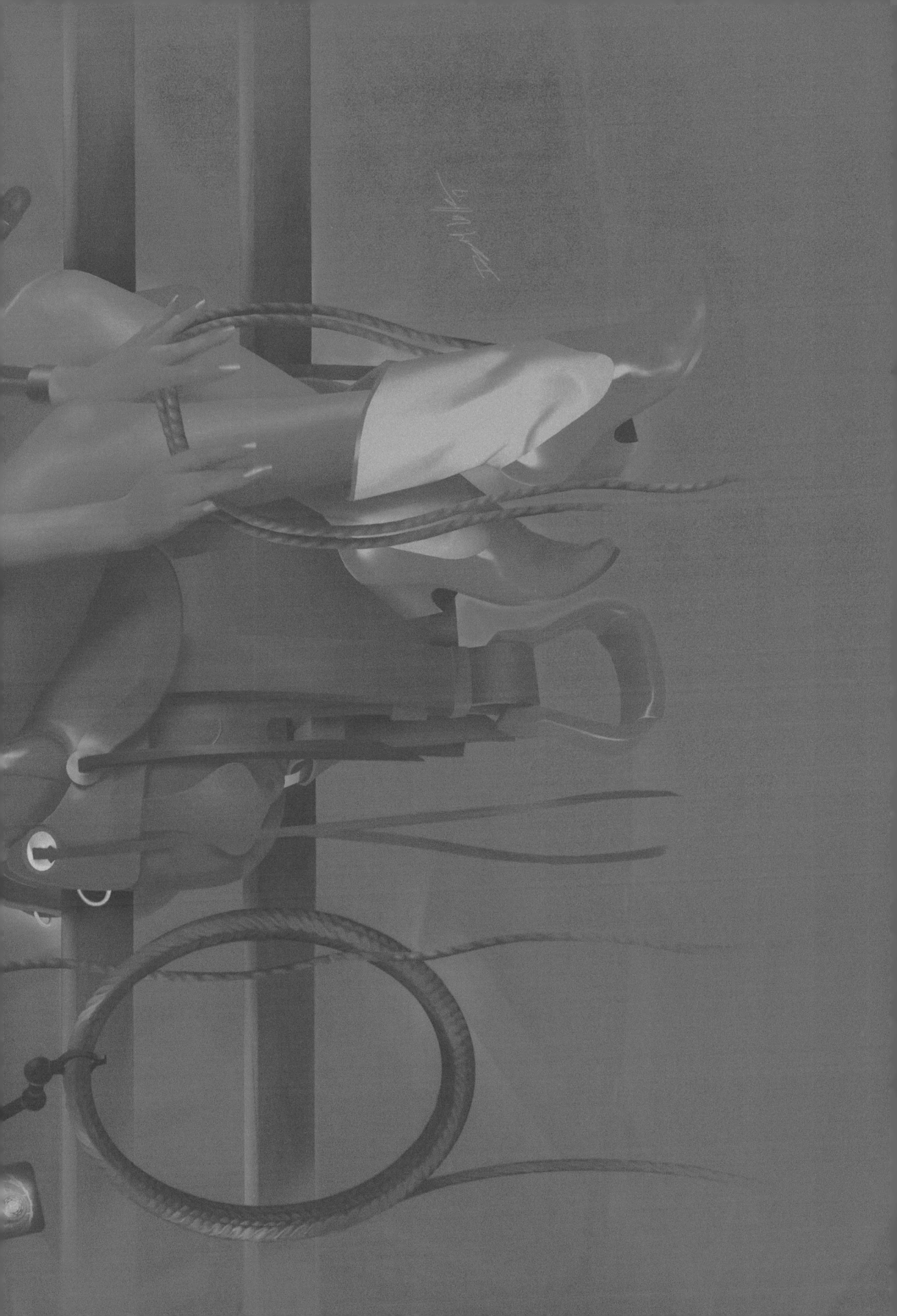

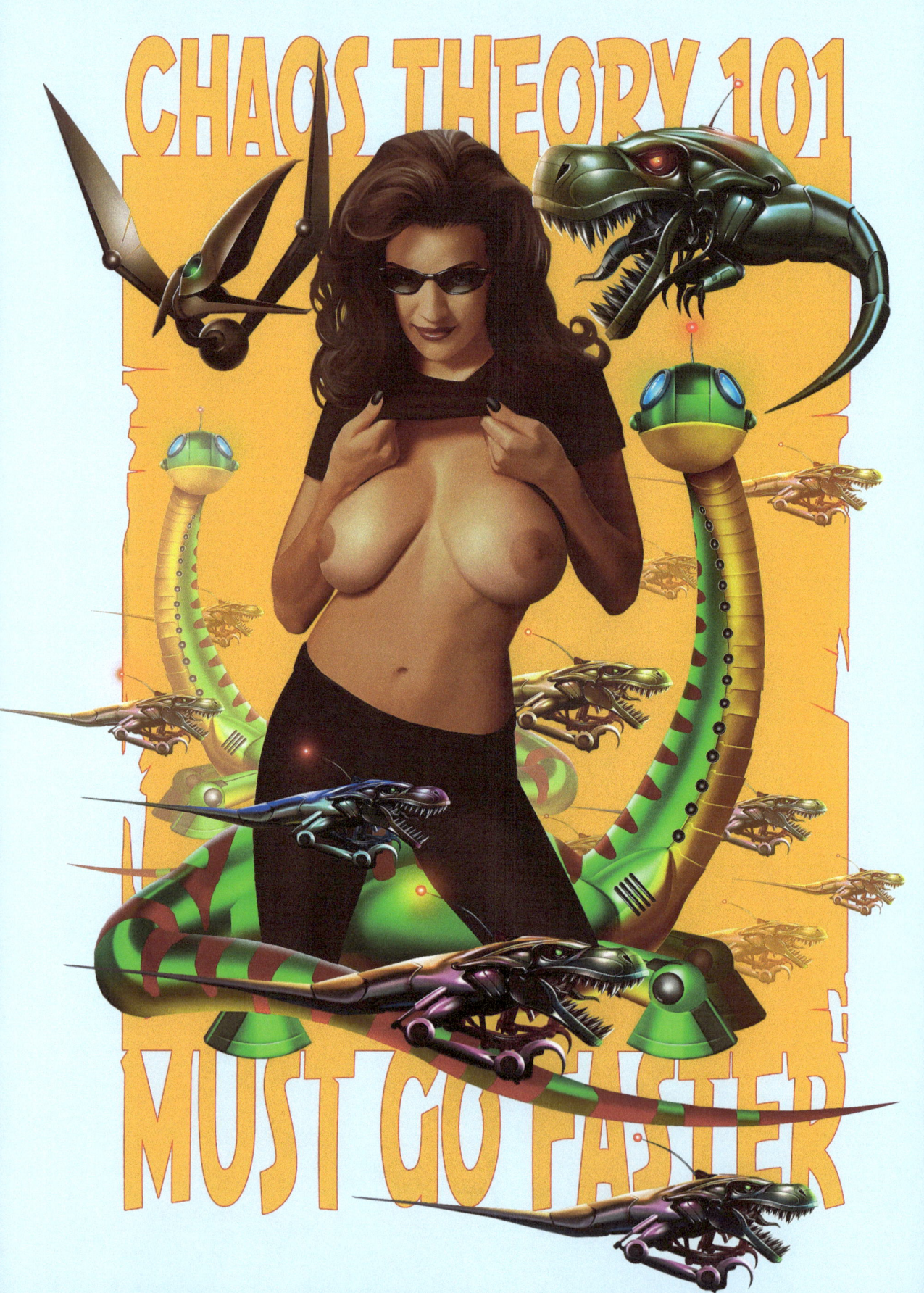

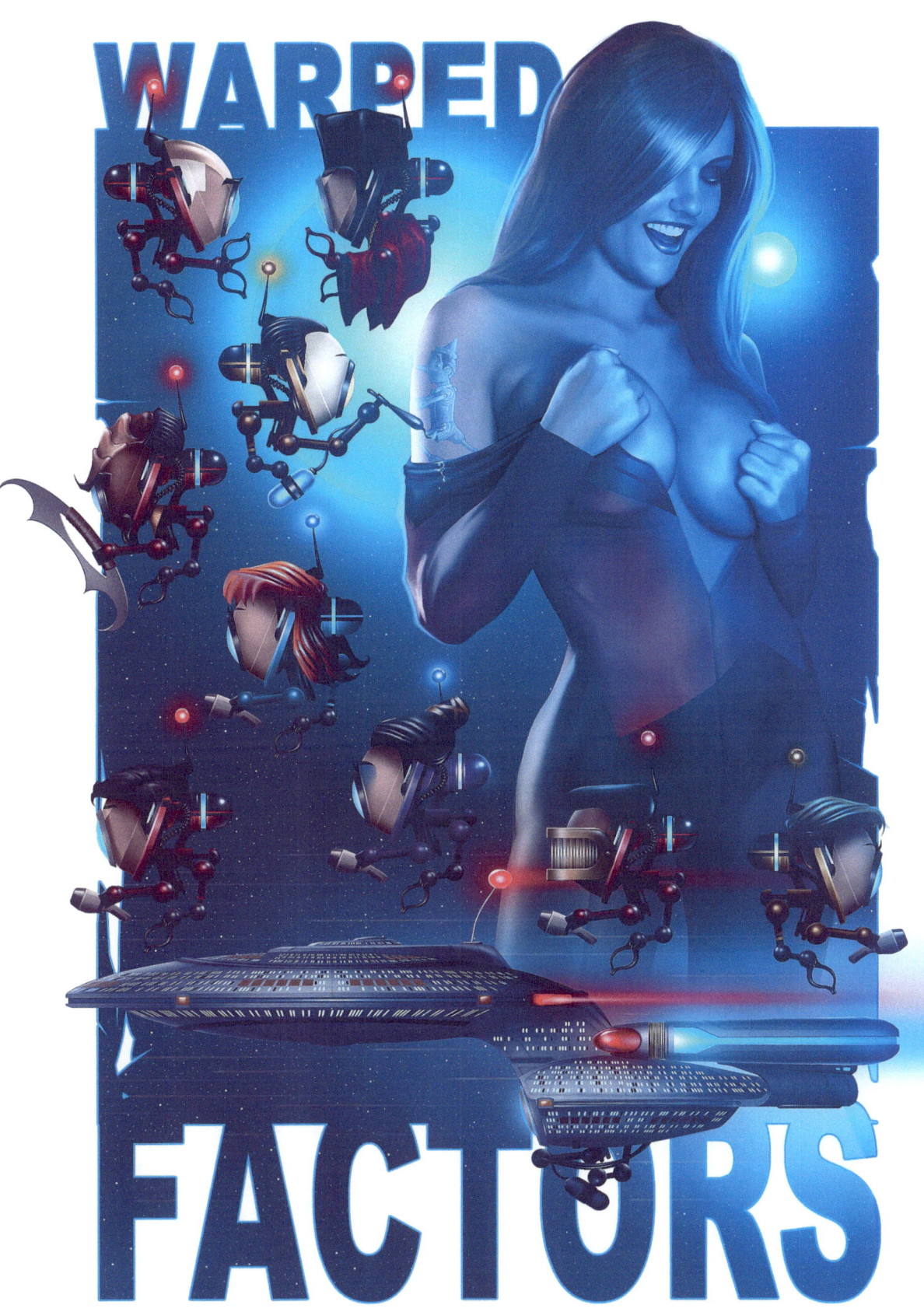

NON-TERRESTRIAL INTELLIGENCE

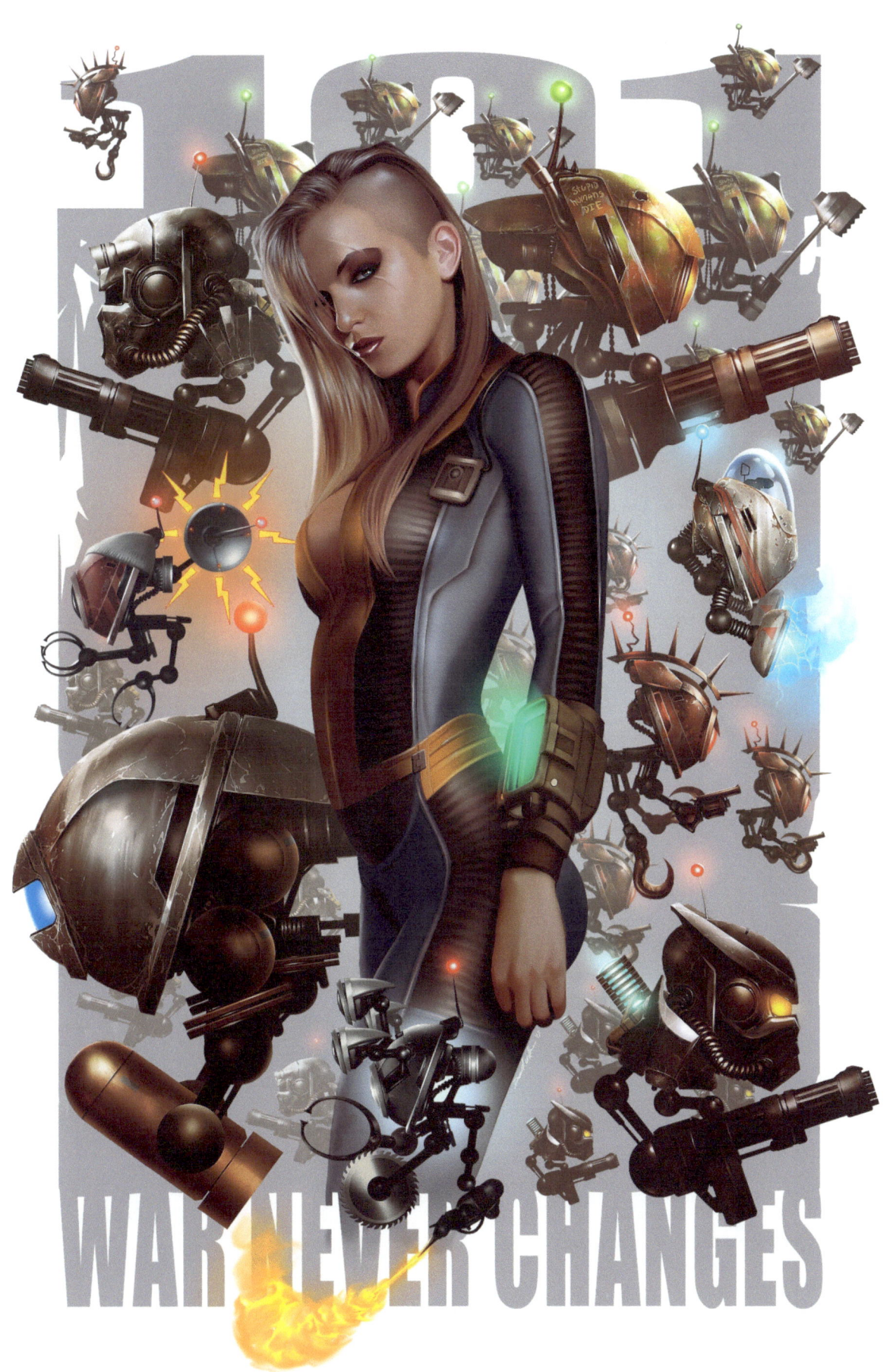

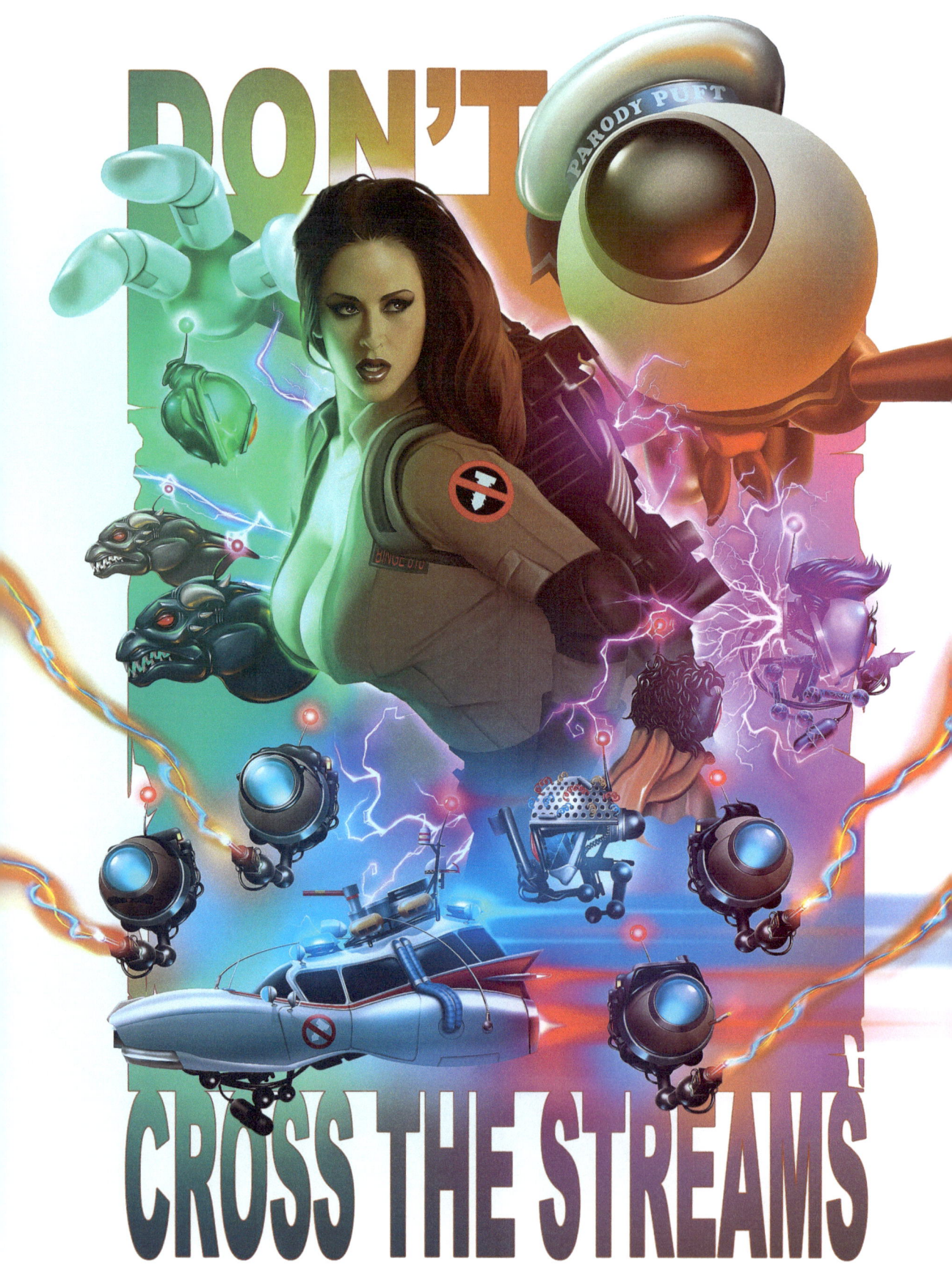

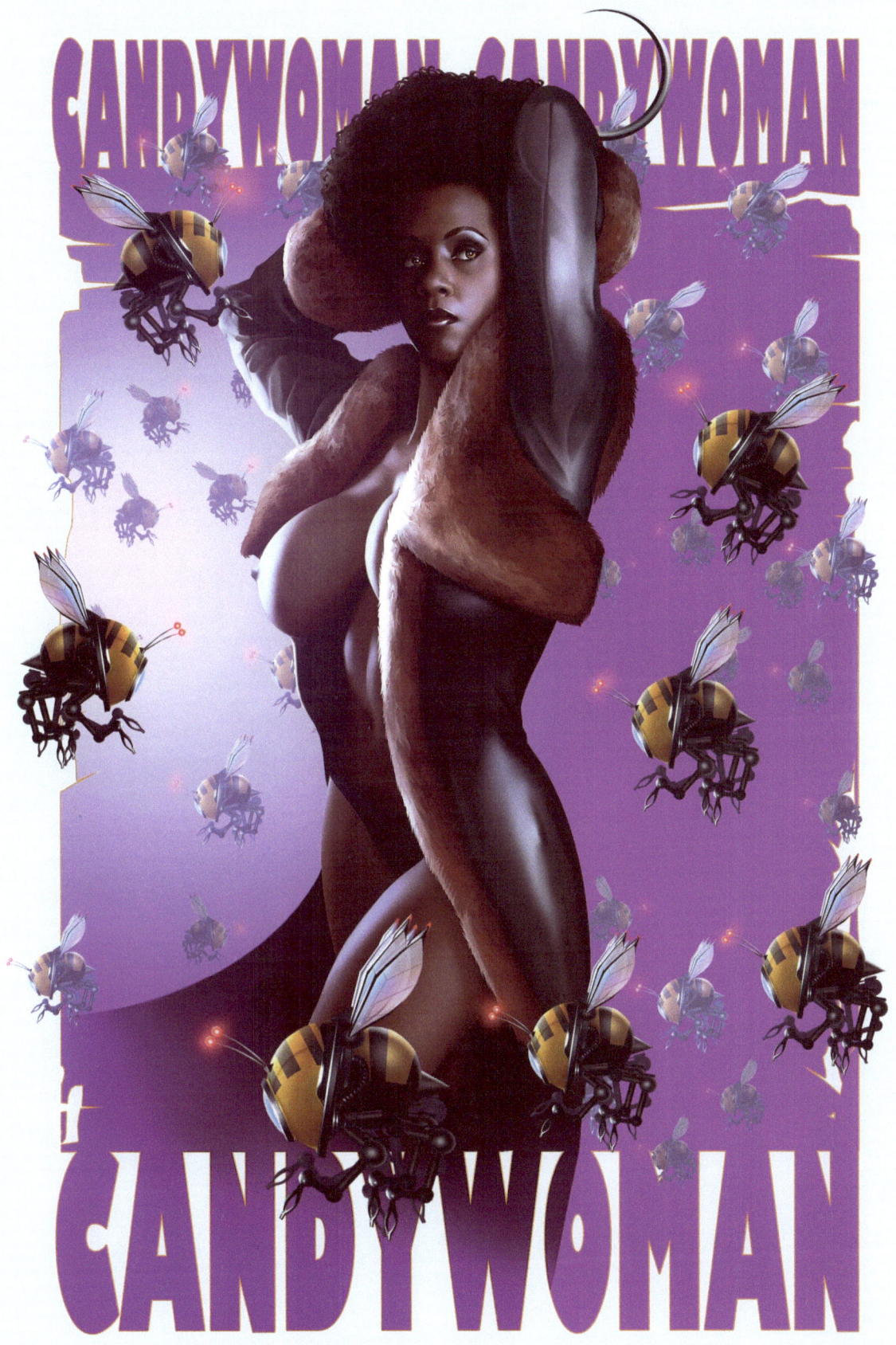

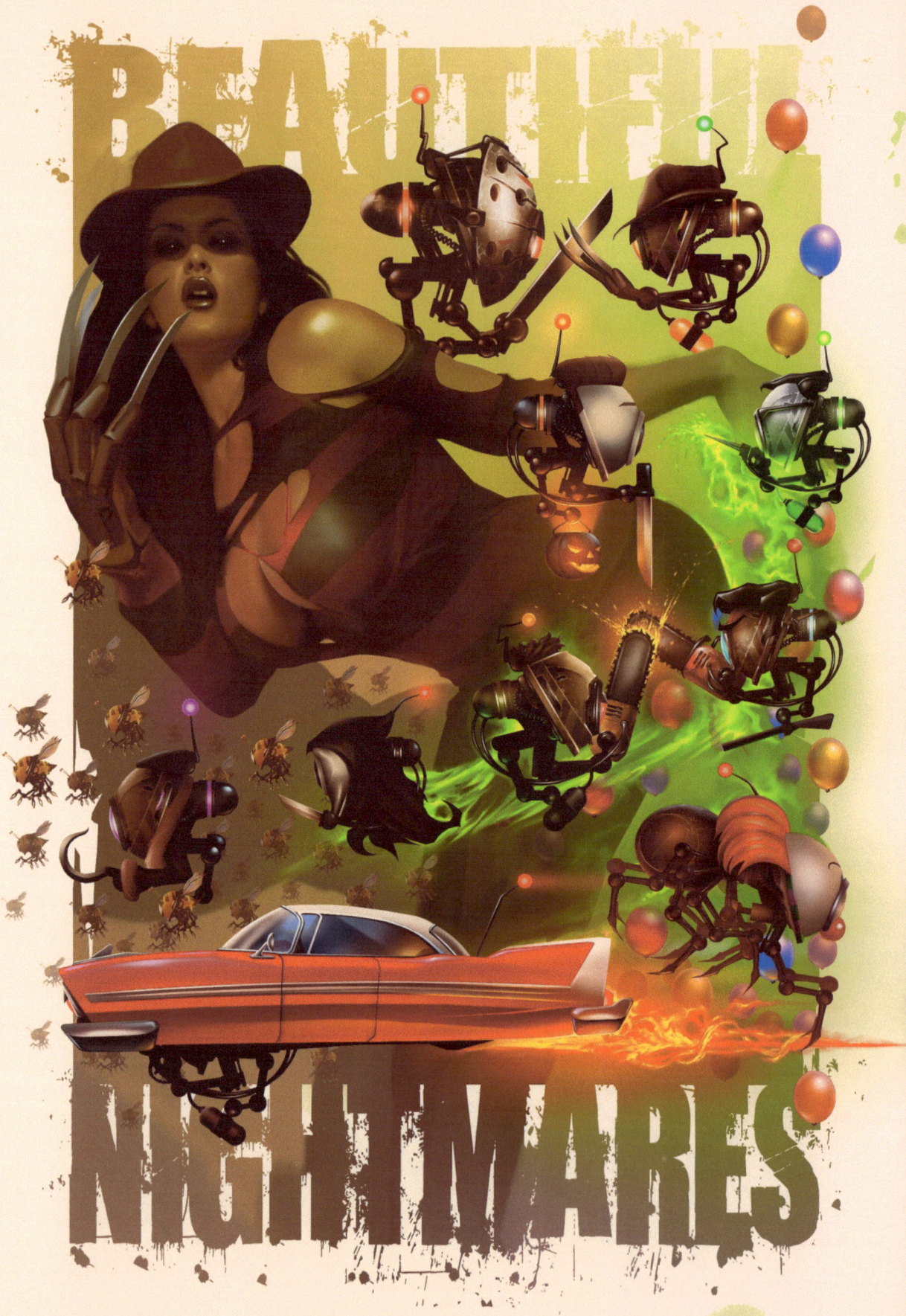

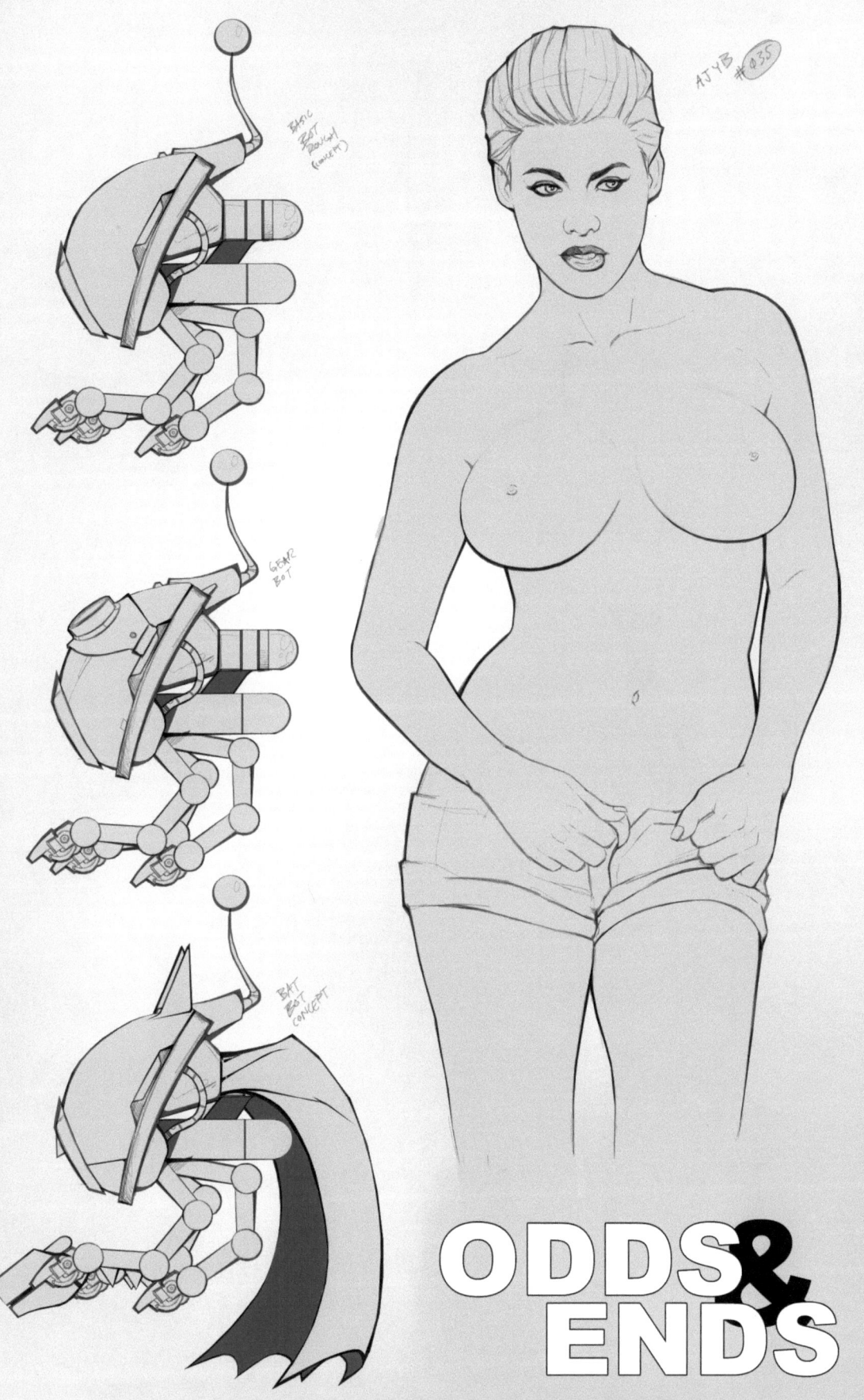

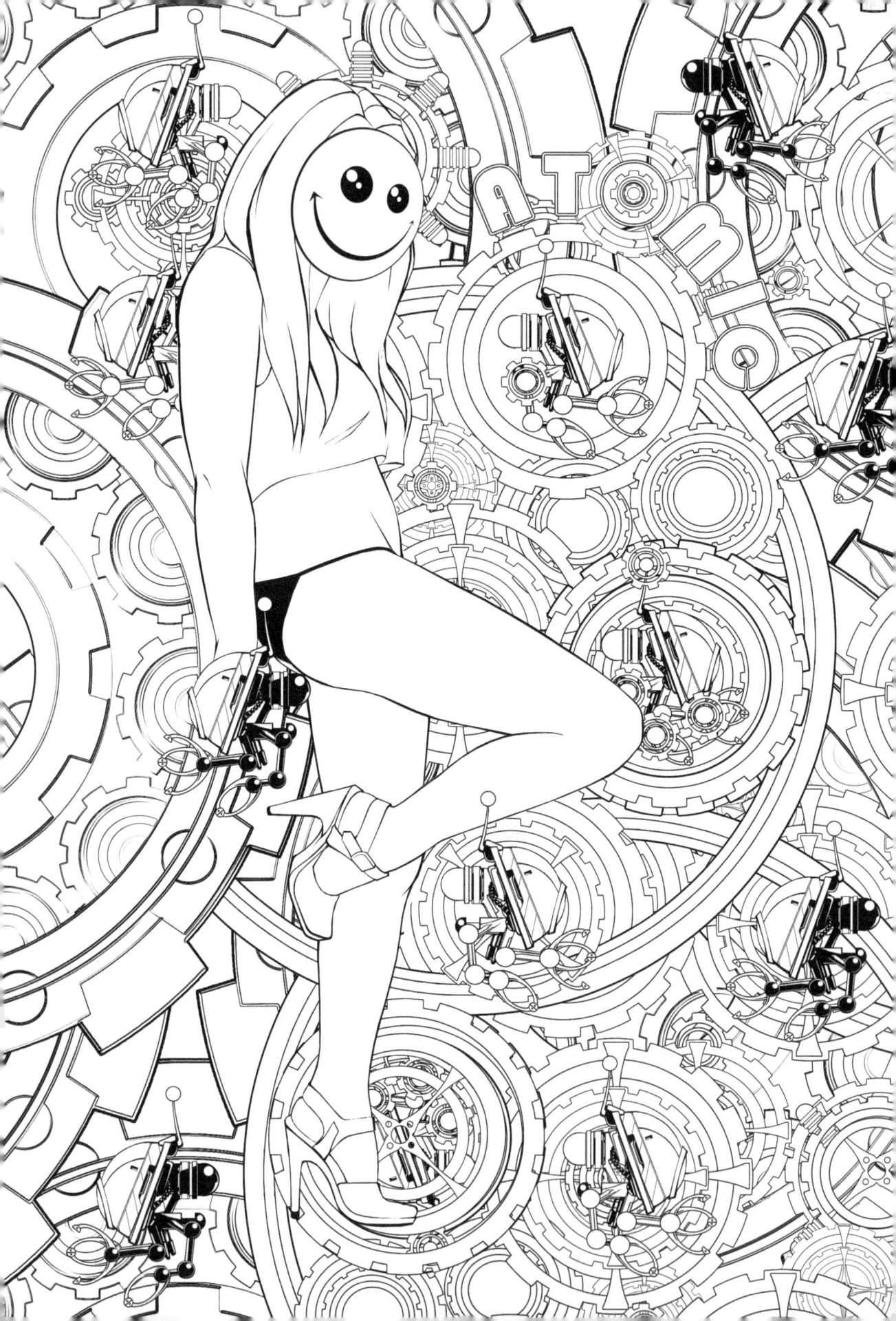

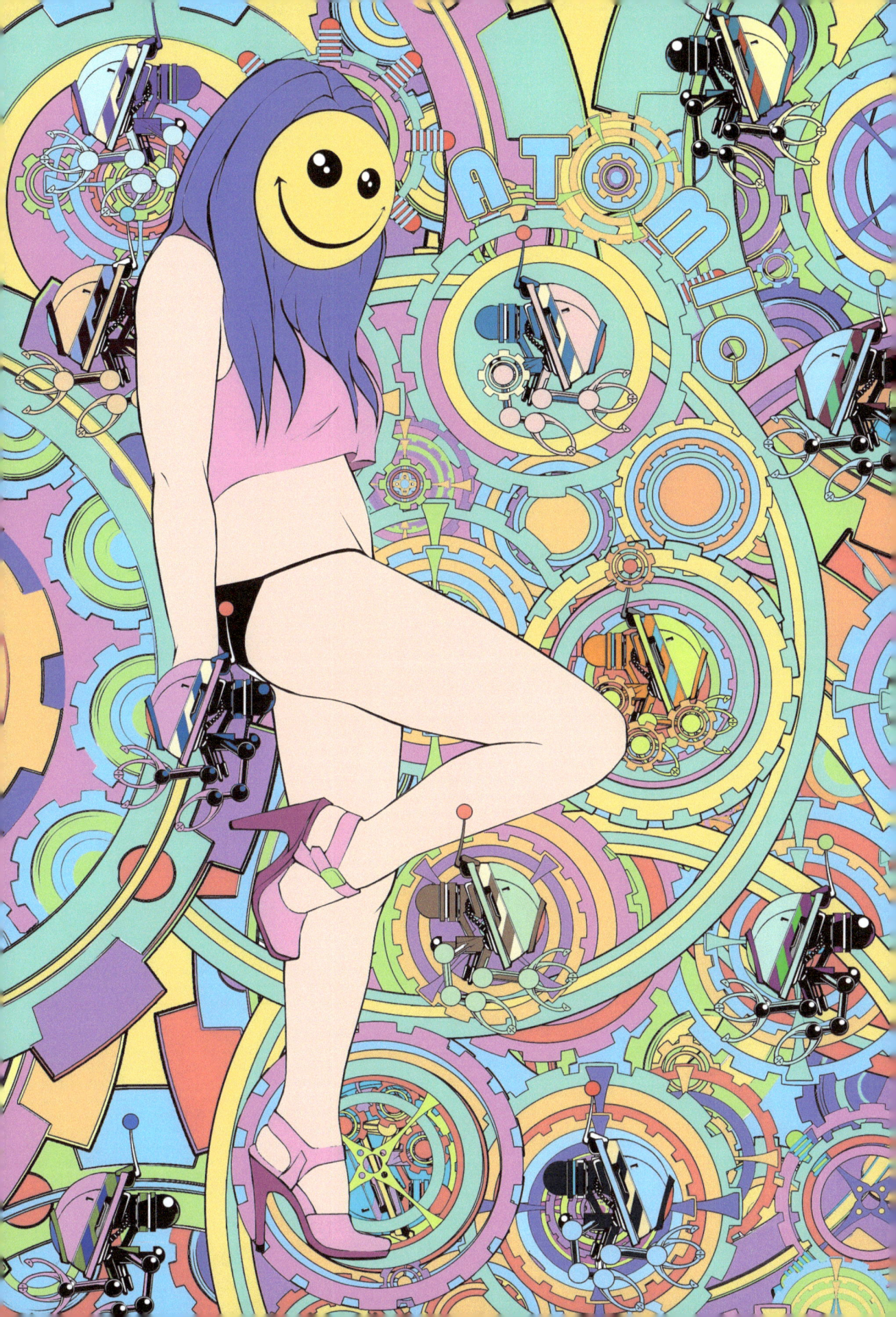

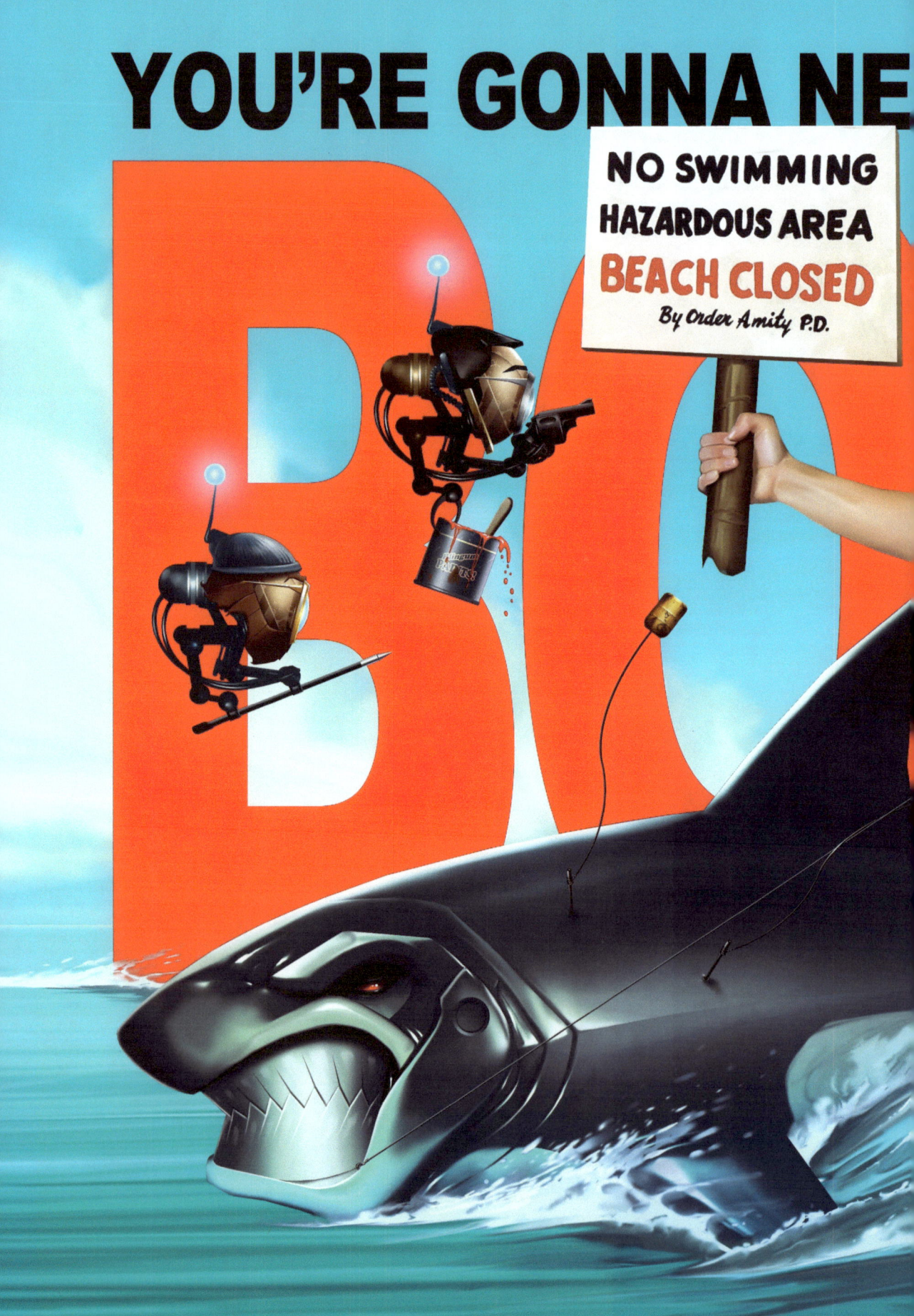

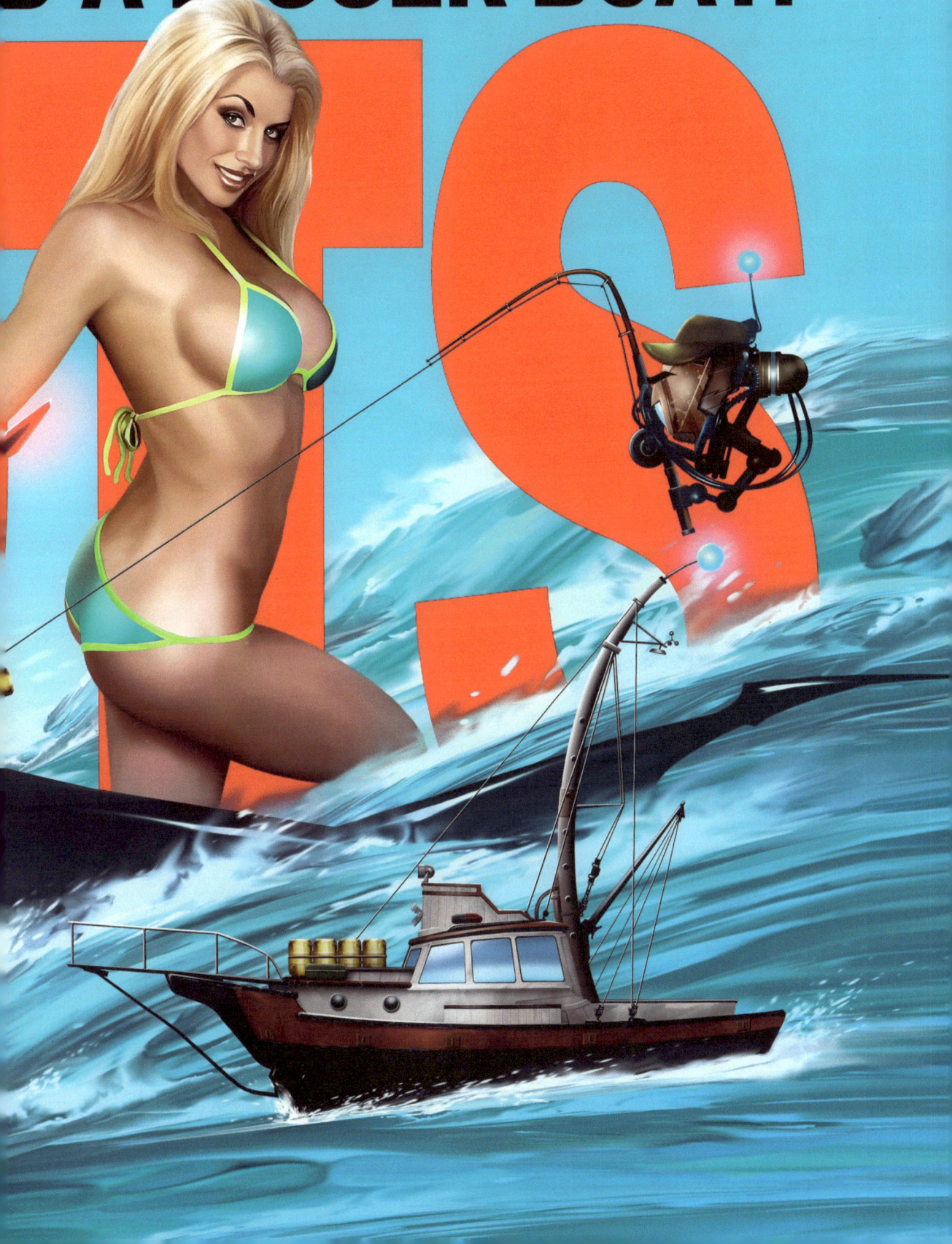

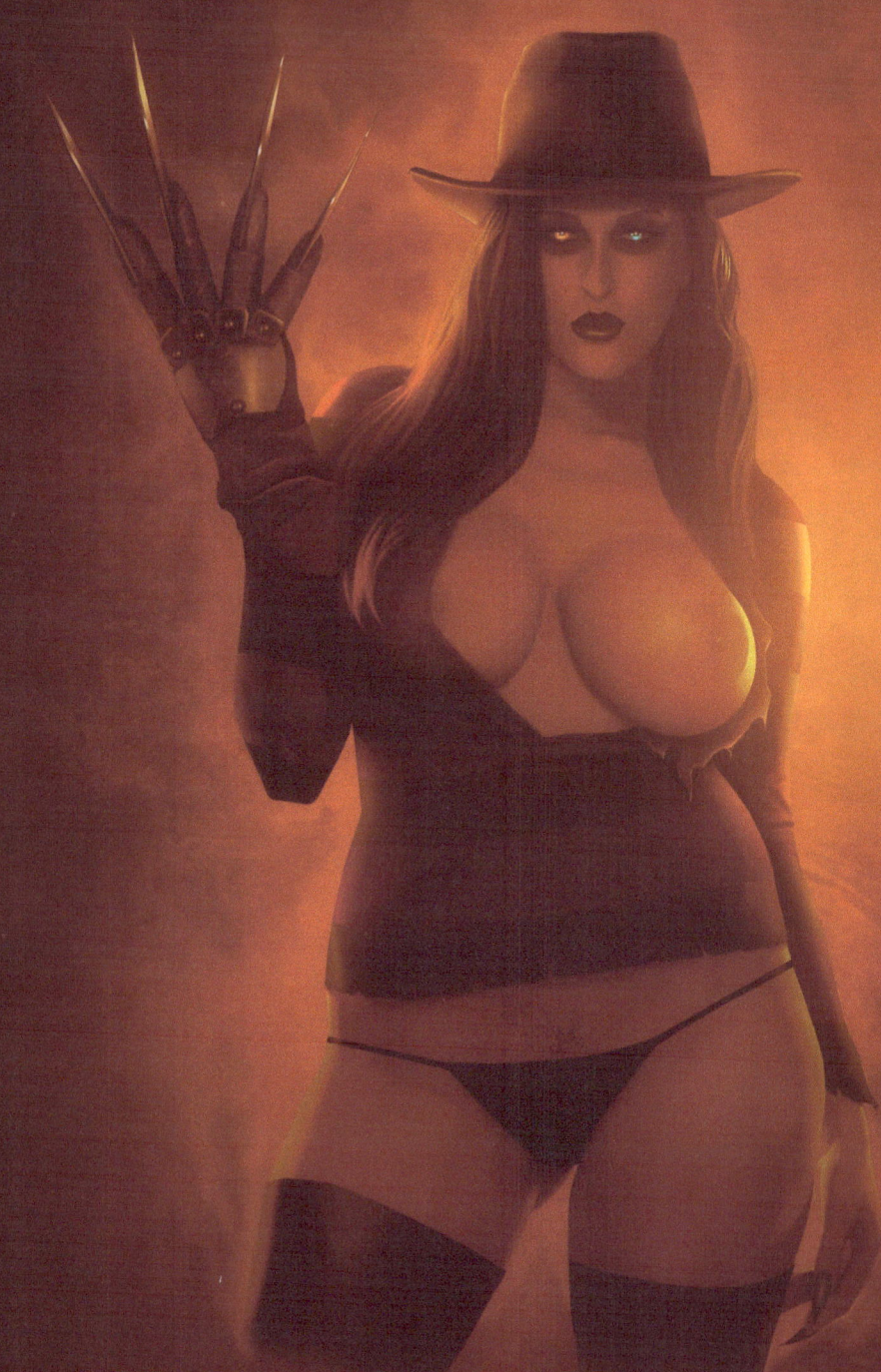

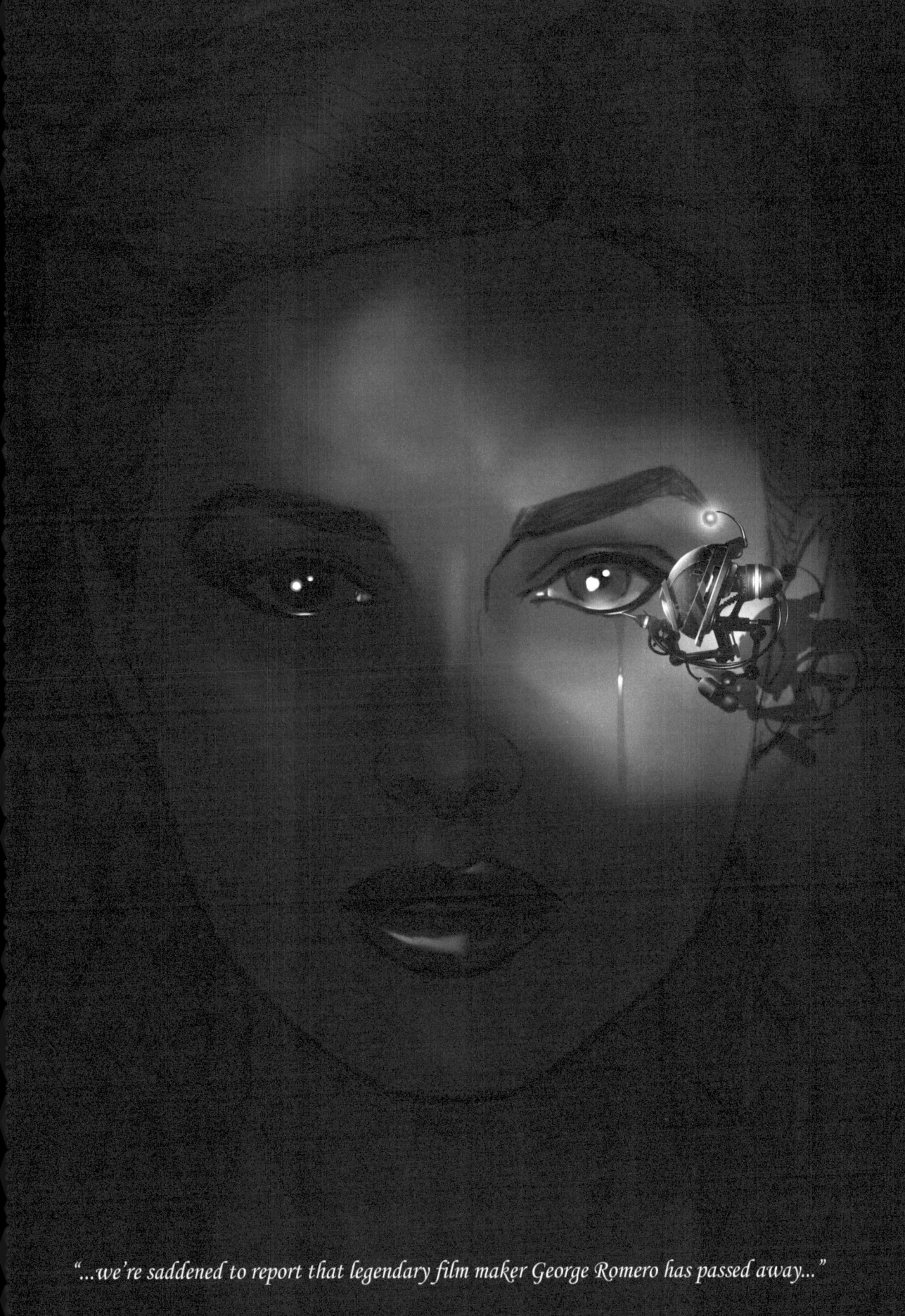
"...we're saddened to report that legendary film maker George Romero has passed away..."

Groovy GLOW STICKS

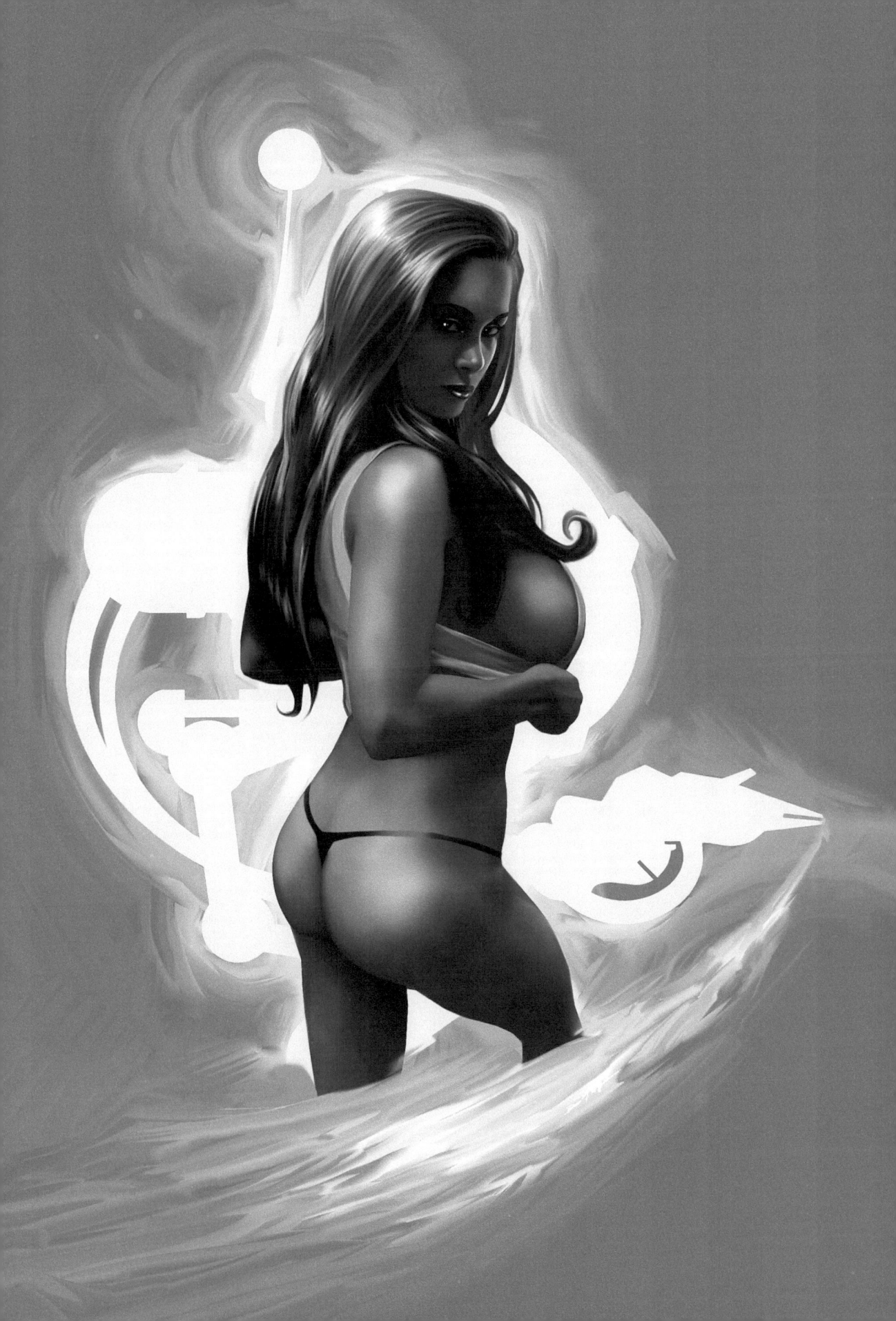

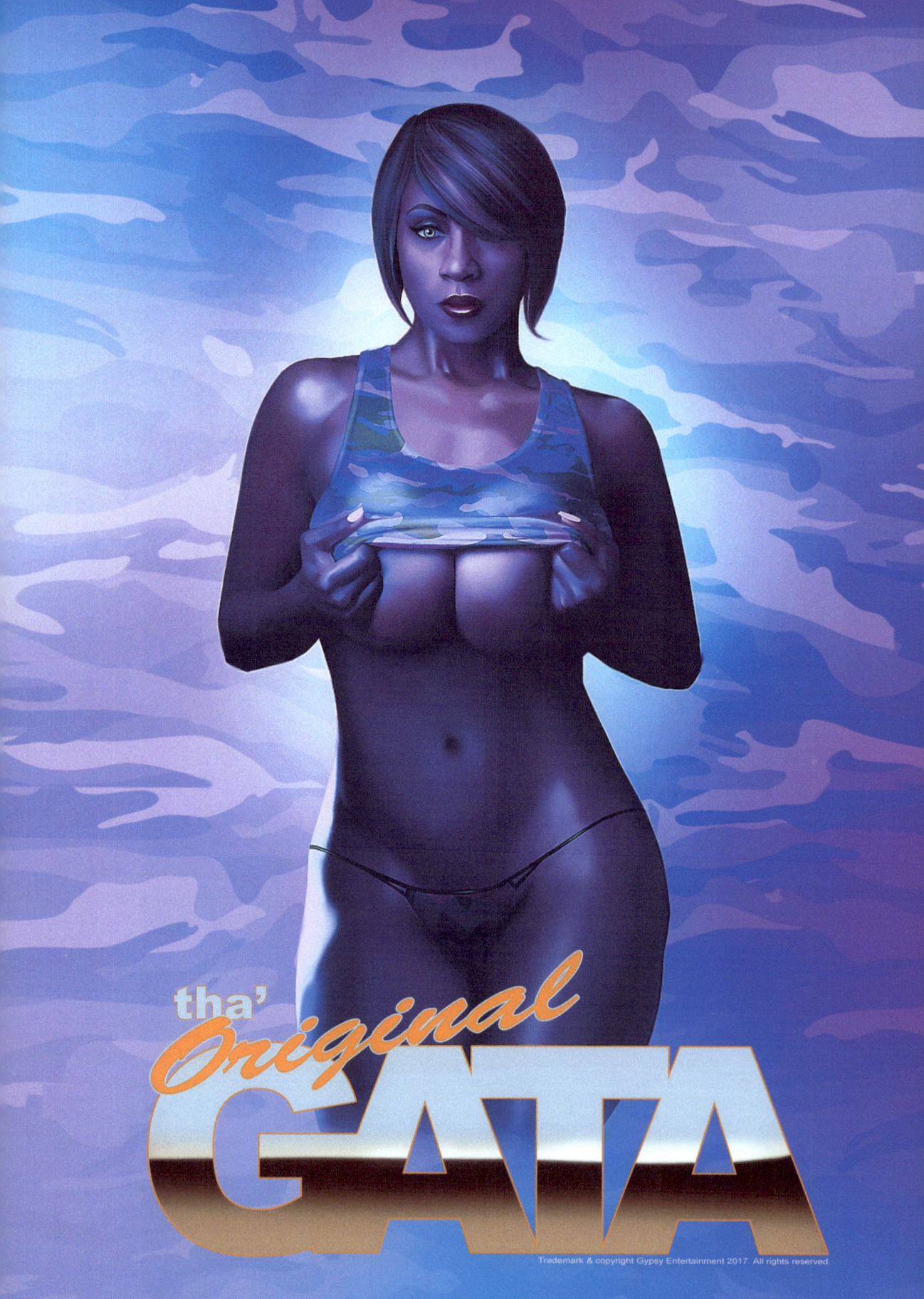

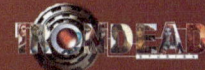

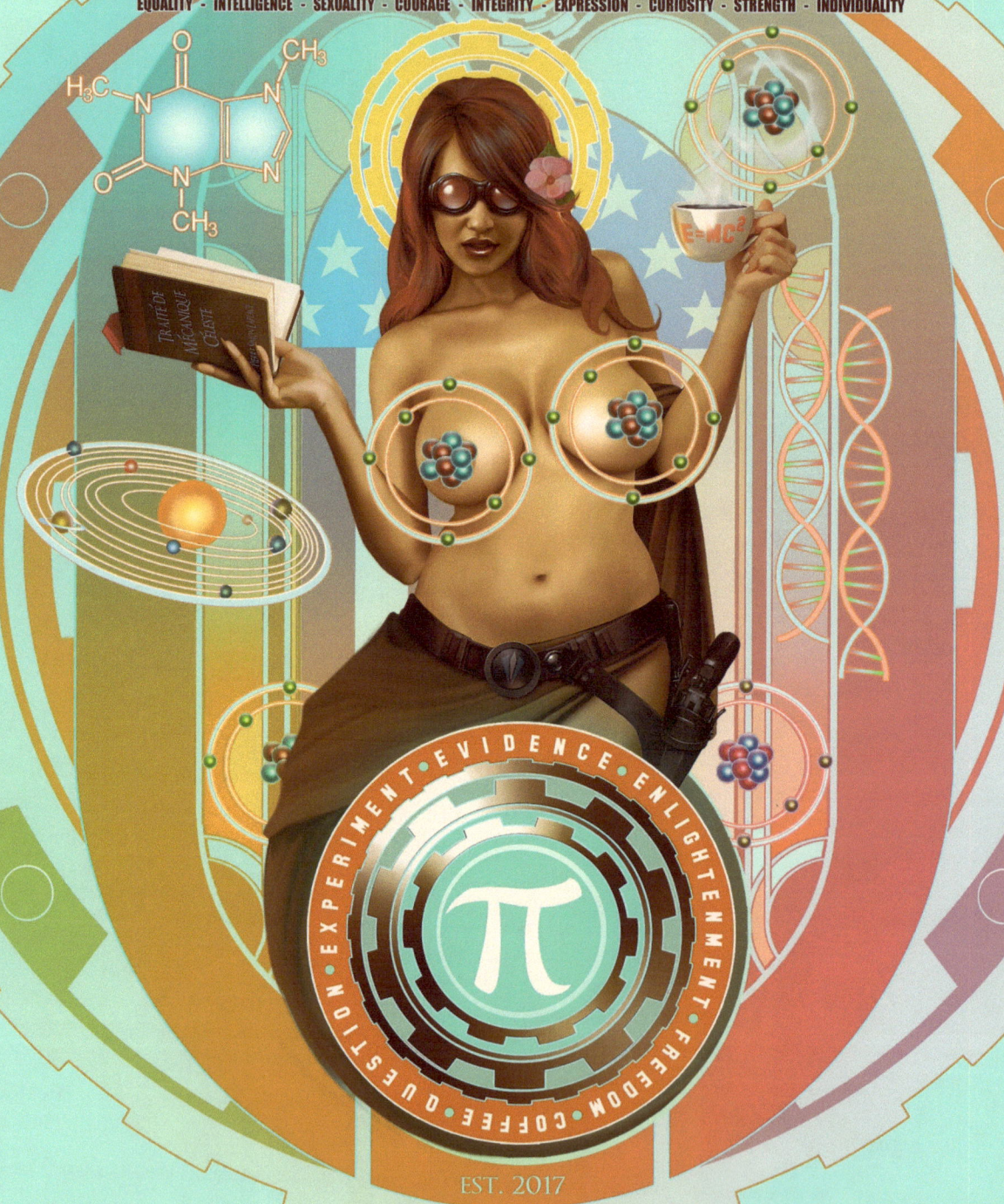

www.ingramcontent.com/pod-product-compliance
Lightning Source LLC
Chambersburg PA
CBHW040411220526
45473CB00004B/1197